Angela Diaz

Ten Things

Every Child With Autism Wishes You Knew

Ellen Notbohm

Ten Things

Every Child With Autism Wishes You Knew

All marketing and publishing rights guaranteed to and reserved by

FUTURE HORIZONS INC.

721 W. Abram Street
Arlington, TX 76013

800-489-0727

817-277-0727

817-277-2270 Fax

Website: www.FHautism.com
E-mail: info@FHautism.com

Cover design and text layout by Matt Mitchell, www.mattmitchelldesign.com

ISBN 1-932565-30-2

What readers say about

Ten Things Every Child With Autism Wishes You Knew

Original article published as

"What Every Child with Autism Wishes You Knew"
Children's Voice, Nov. 2004

"Ten Things Every Child with Autism Wishes You Knew"
South Florida Parenting, Nov. 2004

I immediately thought, "WOW! This is what I have been trying to tell everyone!!" I sure could "see" my son in all that you wrote, and your words gave me more strength to carry on and do all I can to help my son. My own family doesn't understand and I get tired trying to explain it over and over again. Most times they pity us, but I don't want pity or empathy. I want them to get some sense of understanding. [Ten Things] outlines everything beautifully.

Squamish, British Columbia

Super presentation. When [our grandkids] were first tagged with this current "epidemic," I read everything I could get my hands on. Nothing spelled it out as well as you did.

Atlanta, Georgia

Ten Things Every Child with Autism Wishes You Knew *was a lot of help. I cried reading it and kept nodding my head saying . . . true, very true. Once again, it's people like you who make it easier for us to understand what we don't know or ask ourselves.*

Toronto, Ontario

It was very inspiring, educational, uplifting and couldn't have been written at a better time . . . made me more proud to be the mother of a child with autism.

Atlanta, Georgia

From the blogs, bulletin boards and chat groups:

"Wow, really great article. The 'Ohhhh...that's why he does that sometimes' light bulb went on when I read about sensory overload."

"Loved the article. My daughter who is dx with autism will totally agree with it."

"Very well done! (I was actually prepared to hate it.)"

"I am sitting here with tears running down my face. Not sadness or joy—understanding. How I wish I had read something like this five years ago. It took us such a long time to 'learn' these things. I am passing it to my son's teachers and to my mother-in-law who continues to ask when he will outgrow 'it' and be 'normal.'"

"I read this and I just cried and cried. NOW I understand what is happening to our son."

"Clapclapclapclapclapclapclap!"

Now Available!

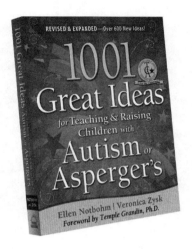

1001 Great Ideas for Teaching and Raising Children with Autism or Asperger's

(with Veronica Zysk)

Winner of *Learning Magazine's* Teacher's Choice Award

"Genuine, commonsense advice that all parents and educators can quickly and easily use!"

—TEMPLE GRANDIN, PH.D., autism expert and author of *The Way I See It*

For Connor and Bryce
because they have done such a good job of raising me

Contents

Preface

When my article "Ten Things Every Child with Autism Wishes You Knew" (a.k.a. "What Every Child with Autism Wishes You Knew") was originally published in November 2004, I could scarcely have anticipated the response. Reader after reader wrote to tell me that the piece should be required reading for all social service workers, teachers and relatives of children with autism. "Just what my daughter would say if she could," said one mother. "Screams wisdom throughout every word and sentence," said another. The article traveled from website to website, around the world: United States, Canada, France, Turkey, Brazil, The Netherlands, Venezuela, Australia, Singapore. As the publication tally crossed the one hundred mark, I was struck by not only the volume but also the diversity of the groups who had found it relevant. Dozens of autism and Asperger's groups did, of course, but also support groups for chronic pain, obesity, assistance dogs, inner ear disorders, home schoolers, church educators, a knitting circle—and a chocolate company! "I have a strong sense that your message crosses over to many special needs," wrote a social worker in the Midwest.

"Ten Things" was almost taking on a life of its own; why exactly was it resonating so loudly? I decided that it was coming from the fact that the piece spoke with a child's voice, a voice that goes largely unheard in the rising uproar about autism. It's a good, productive, welcome uproar. But what could be more ironic than the fact that the subjects of the uproar are widely exemplified by the inability to express and advocate for themselves. I had seen several articles that took related approaches: ten things teachers want parents to know, or what mothers wish their children's teachers knew, what ASD dads need to know. I asked myself, who speaks for the child?

You do, came the self-reply.

My grandmother liked to say that when you talk to yourself, you always get the answer you want. The answer was that I felt very, very fortunate that Bryce's "voice" had been heard, thanks to very committed teamwork, and that I ardently wanted his level of success to be the norm, not the exception. My article, and now this book, flows from that.

It does require some level of presumption to think that any one of us can get inside someone else's head and speak for them. I hope I can be forgiven for this, in the light of the overwhelming need to understand the world as the child with autism experiences it. It falls on us to grant legitimacy and worth to their different way of thinking and navigating the world. It demands that we give voice to their thoughts and feelings, even when that voice is wordless. If we don't, the legacy of our children's autism will be opportunities untouched, gifts forever undiscovered. They are our call to action.

It begins . . .

As the mother of a very young child with autism, one of the first things I learned was that on some days, the only predictable thing about it is the unpredictability; the only consistent attribute—the inconsistency. There is little argument on any level that autism is baffling, even to those who spend their lives around it. The child who lives with autism may look "normal," but his behavior can be perplexing and downright difficult.

Autism was once thought an "incurable disorder," but that notion is crumbling in the face of knowledge and understanding that is increasing even as you read this. Every day, individuals with autism are showing us that they can overcome, compensate for and otherwise manage many of autism's most challenging aspects as part of their fulfilling and dynamic lives. Some even seek to do away with the notion of "cure." In a widely read *New York Times* article in December 2004, Jack Thomas, a 10th grader with Asperger's Syndrome, got the world's attention by stating: "We don't have a disease, so we can't be 'cured.' This is just the way we are."

Jack and I are on the same page here: when "neuro-typicals" frame the challenges of autism in neuro-typical terms, they unwittingly close the door to the kind of alternative thinking that has everything to do with how far those with ASD can go.

This is the mantra of my column, "Postcards from the Road Less Traveled" (*Autism Asperger's Digest*). In a 2005 column, I asked parents to jot down brief descriptions of some of their child's most challenging behaviors, and then to rephrase them in the positive. Is the child stand-offish, or able to entertain herself and work well independently? Is she reckless, or adventuresome and willing to try new experiences? Is she obsessively neat, or does she have outstanding organizational skills? Does she pester you with endless questions, or does she have a curiosity about her world as well as tenacity and persistence? Why do we try to fix the kid who "perseverates" but admire the one who "perseveres?" Both are forms of the same word meaning "refuses to stop."

Here's the one I hate the most: Does your child "suffer from autism," or does he "live with autism?"

Choose "life" over "suffering."

The column is called "Postcards from the Road Less Traveled" because my editor, Veronica Zysk, and I thought the connection to Robert Frost's poem was very apt.

> *Two roads diverged in a wood, and I —*
> *I took the one less traveled by,*
> *And that has made all the difference.*

One reader disagreed: "Postcards are from people who are having a good time on a trip. I'm not sure if that's what you want to portray."

I think postcards are so much more than that. They let loved ones know you've arrived at a certain place safely. They say, "I am thinking of you even though I am far away," and they share the sights you are seeing with that someone so they can be with you across the distance. They may recount trip-related woes and how you resolved them, hopefully with a bit of humor.

So my answer to that reader is yes, that is exactly what I want to portray, in the column, in this book, and in all my dialogue with parents and teachers. I *am* having a good time on this trip. The trip has been fueled by hope, possibility, undreamed-of accomplishments (his, mine and my whole family's) and "return on investment." But we did not start out from there.

We started with a basically sweet-tempered but nonverbal child who would lapse into baffling episodes of hair-tearing, cat-scratching, furniture-throwing violence; who wore clothes only when socially necessary and who physically backed away from many classroom and playtime activities with his hands over his ears; who laughed at all the wrong times and didn't seem to experience pain or cold in a typical way.

Bryce was identified with autism by a public school early intervention team at the age of three. I went through the five stages of grief in the time it took to end the initial meeting. My older son had been identified two years earlier with AD/HD. I already knew about the therapies, the social challenges, the never-ending vigilance—and the exhaustion.

Raw fear motivated me in the beginning. I could not bear to imagine Bryce's fate as an adult if I did not do everything within my power to equip him to live in a world where I would not always be around. I could not rid my head of words like "prison" and "homeless." Not for a nanosecond did it occur to me to leave his future to the professionals or to the ephemeral idea that "he might outgrow it." His very quality of life was at stake, and failure was simply not an option. This is what got me out of bed every morning and drove me to take the actions I did for him.

Jump a few years ahead with me now to the turn of the century. At the school assembly, adorable first graders step to the microphone one after another to answer the question: what would you like to be in the new millennium? "A soccer star!" is one popular response. "A pop singer!" "A race car driver!" "Cartoon artist, veterinarian, firefighter!"

Bryce has considered the question carefully: "I think I'd just like to be a grown-up."

Applause breaks out and the principal speaks deliberately. "The world would be a better place," he says, "if more people aspired to what Bryce aspires to."

Here is the gist of what I know to be true. Your child's autism does not mean that he, you and your family will not lead full, joyous, meaningful lives. You may be scared, but dare yourself to believe this...with a caveat. How much of that full measure we achieve with our kids is greatly dependent upon the choices we make for and about them given their individuality and uncommon character. A memorable passage from Nora Ephron's story *Heartburn* has the protagonist asserting that when your dream breaks into a million pieces, you can either fall apart, or you can go get yourself a new dream.

Some of you will be reading this as newcomers to the world of autism. To you I say: autism itself is not awful. Not understanding it, not having people around you who understand it, not getting the help that is surely out there for your child—that can be very awful. You are at the beginning of your journey, and we won't deny that it's a long one, will we? And you would not begin any long journey without first learning a little bit about your route. That's what this book is for—to point out some basic signposts you will likely pass along the way, so that when you do, they will have a familiar look to them and be less foreign and frightening.

Some of you are already well-acquainted with the challenges of autism; sport a few scars too, I'll bet. This book can speak for you and your child when so many need to hear your message: teachers, parents, siblings, in-laws, babysitters, coaches, bus drivers, peer parents, friends of siblings, clergy, neighbors. Pass it around. Watch the dominos fall.

This book will equip those around our children with simple understanding of autism's most basic elements. That understanding has a tremendous impact on the children's ability to journey towards productive, independent adulthood. Autism is an extremely complex disorder but throughout my experience, I saw its myriad characteristics fall into four fundamental areas: sensory processing challenges, speech/language delays and impairments, the elusive social interaction skills and whole child/self-esteem issues. All are crucial. Here's why:

> *Sensory processing challenges:* It's inescapable. A child cannot be expected to absorb cognitive or social learning, or even "behave," when his environment is a constant bombardment of unpleasant sensations and nasty surprises. Your brain filters thousands of multiple-sensory inputs (what you see, what you hear, what you smell, etc.) simultaneously, but his does not. It can provoke the equivalent of twenty-four-hour "road rage" as all those signals jam hopelessly in the brain stem. Think of how you feel trapped in the stifling fumes and racket of traffic with no ability to affect your situation.

> *Speech/language delays and impairments:* Without adequate means of expression, needs and wants will remain unmet. The inevitable result is anger and frustration, not learning and growing. The ability to com-

municate, whether through spoken language, pictures, signing/semaphore or assistive technology, is bedrock.

Social interaction skills: Elusive and ephemeral, these skills change from culture to culture, and from setting to setting within a culture. But the lack of them can isolate a child to a devastating degree. The child with autism, who truly doesn't "get it," paddles against a brutal current in first comprehending, then executing.

Whole child/self-esteem issues: Every last person on the planet is a package deal. We want to be accepted and appreciated for what we are as a whole, not a bundle of traits and quirks to be cherry-picked at will by others. The child with autism does need skilled guidance to achieve a comfortable place in the larger world, but working toward that goal with positive energy and optimism is not the same as "fixing" the child. They already possess much that can be celebrated; we must now go out and love and guide them with the same acceptance of whole self we want for ourselves.

Bryce's successes are firmly rooted in that solid sense of self-esteem, his hard-won comfort with his physical environment and his ever-expanding ability to express himself. With those pieces in place, social and cognitive learning followed. As his life became easier, so did mine. Each passing year brought deeply gratifying triumphs: the day he swam to a trophy finish in a city-wide swim meet, the day he sang and danced his way through *Charlie and the Chocolate Factory* as Grandpa Joe, the day he rode his two-wheeler for the first time, the time we worried no one would come to his birthday party and forty people showed up, his elation at making it through his first Scout campout, and his utter euphoria after successfully working up the nerve to ask the girl he'd admired since kindergarten to dance at the sock hop.

And the truth is, in time I came to realize that I would not change him even if I could. I wouldn't take his autism away. I wouldn't have him be anything other than exactly what he was.

Though the four elements we've just discussed may be common to many children with autism, keep in mind that it is a spectrum disorder: no two (or ten or twenty) children with autism will be completely alike. Every child will be at a different point on the spectrum. And, just as importantly, every parent, teacher and caregiver will be at a different point in their understanding of the spectrum. Child or adult, each will have a unique set of needs. Like the millions of pixels that comprise a television image, each person involved is a complicated composite. That's why there is no single recipe for success and why guiding, educating and appreciating the child with autism will be a continual work-in-progress. There will be little time off for complacency. The famous opera diva Beverly Sills, mother of two special needs children, once said: "There is no shortcut to anyplace worth going." True—but there is the joy of discovery in the journey. The guidebook is in your hands. Let's get started.

Here are ten things every child with autism wishes you knew.

I am first and foremost a child. I have autism. I am not primarily "autistic."

My autism is only one aspect of my total character. It does not define me as a person. Are you a person with thoughts, feelings, and many talents, or are you individualized by one trait? Are you fat (overweight), myopic (wear glasses) or klutzy (uncoordinated, not good at sports)? Those may be things that I see first when I meet you, but they are not necessarily what you are all about.

As an adult, you have some control over how you define yourself. If you want to single out a single characteristic, you can make that known. As a child, I am still unfolding. Neither you nor I yet know what I may be capable of. Defining me by one characteristic runs the danger of setting up an expectation that may be too low. And if I get a sense that you don't think I "can do it," my natural response will be: Why try?

My sensory perceptions are disordered.

This means that the ordinary sights, sounds, smells, tastes and touches of every day that you may not even notice can be downright painful for me. The very environment in which I have to live often seems hostile. I may appear withdrawn or belligerent to you but I am really just trying to defend myself. Here is why a simple trip to the grocery store may be hell for me.

My hearing may be hyper-acute. Dozens of people are talking at once. The loudspeaker booms today's special. Musak whines from the sound system. Cash registers beep and cough, a coffee grinder is chugging. The meat cutter screeches, babies wail, carts creak, the fluorescent lighting hums. My brain can't filter all the input and I'm in overload!

My sense of smell may be highly sensitive. The fish at the meat counter isn't quite fresh, the guy standing next to us hasn't showered today, the deli is handing out sausage samples, the baby in line ahead of us has a poopy diaper, they're mopping up pickles on aisle three with ammonia—I can't sort it all out. I am dangerously nauseated.

Because I am visually oriented, this may be my first sense to become overstimulated. The fluorescent light is not only too bright, it buzzes and hums. The room seems to pulsate and it hurts my eyes. The pulsating light bounces off everything and distorts what I am seeing—the space seems to be constantly changing. There are too many items for me to be able to focus (I may compensate with "tunnel vision"), like glares from windows, moving fans on the ceiling, and so many bodies in constant motion. All this affects my vestibular and proprioceptive senses, and now I can't even tell where my body is in space.

Please remember to distinguish between
won't (I choose not to)
and can't (I am not able to).

It isn't that I don't listen to instructions. It's that I can't understand you. When you call to me from across the room, this is what I hear: "*&^%$#@, Billy. #$%^*&^%$&*." Instead, approach me and speak directly to me in plain words: "Please put your book in your desk, Billy. It's time to go to lunch." This tells me what you want me to do and what is going to happen next. Now it is much easier for me to comply.

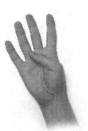

I am a concrete thinker.
This means I interpret language
very literally.

   It's very confusing for me when you say, "Hold your horses, cowboy!" when what you really mean is, "Please stop running." Don't tell me something is a "piece of cake" when there is no dessert in sight and what you really mean is, "This will be easy for you to do." When you say, "It's pouring cats and dogs," I see pets coming out of a pitcher. Please just tell me, "It's raining very hard."

   Idioms, puns, nuances, double entendres, inference, metaphors, allusions and sarcasm are usually lost on me.

very
literal

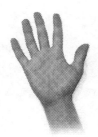

Please be patient with my limited vocabulary.

It's hard for me to tell you what I need when I don't know the words to describe my feelings. I may be hungry, frustrated, frightened or confused but right now those words are beyond my ability to express. Be alert for body language, withdrawal, agitation or other signs that something is wrong.

Or, there's a flip side to this: I may sound like a little professor or movie star, rattling off words or whole scripts well beyond my developmental age. These are messages I have memorized from the world around me to compensate for my language deficits because I know I am expected to respond when spoken to. They may come from books, television, or the speech of other people. It is called "echolalia." I don't necessarily understand the context or the terminology I'm using. I just know that it gets me off the hook for coming up with a reply.

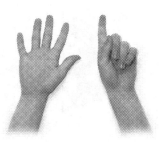

Because language is so difficult for me, I am very visually oriented.

Please show me how to do something rather than just telling me. And please be prepared to show me many times. Lots of consistent repetition helps me learn.

A visual schedule is extremely helpful as I move through my day. Like your day-timer, it relieves me of the stress of having to remember what comes next, makes for smooth transition between activities and helps me manage my time and meet your expectations. Here's a great website for learning more about visual schedules:

www.cesa7.k12.wi.us/sped/autism/structure/str11.htm

I won't lose the need for a visual schedule as I get older, but my "level of representation" may change. Before I can read, I need a visual schedule with photographs or simple drawings. As I get older, a combination of words and pictures may work, and later still, just words.

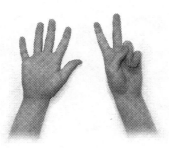

Please focus and build on what I can do rather than what I can't do.

Like any other human, I can't learn in an environment where I'm constantly made to feel that I'm not good enough and that I need "fixing." Trying anything new when I am almost sure to be met with criticism, however "constructive," becomes something to be avoided. Look for my strengths and you will find them. There is more than one right way to do most things.

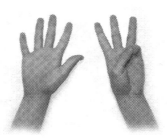

Help me with social interactions.

It may look like I don't want to play with the other kids on the playground, but sometimes it's just that I simply do not know how to start a conversation or enter a play situation. If you can encourage other children to invite me to join them at kickball or shooting baskets, I might be delighted to be included.

I do best in structured play activities that have a clear beginning and end. I don't know how to read facial expressions, body language or the emotions of others, so I appreciate ongoing coaching in proper social responses. For example, if I laugh when Emily falls off the slide, it's not that I think it's funny. It's that I don't know the proper response. Teach me to ask, "Are you okay?"

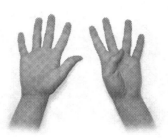

Try to identify what triggers my meltdowns.

Meltdowns, blow-ups, tantrums or whatever you want to call them are even more horrid for me than they are for you. They occur because one or more of my senses has gone into overload.   If you can figure out why my meltdowns occur, they can be prevented.   Keep a log noting times, settings, people, and activities.   A pattern may emerge.

Try to remember that all behavior is a form of communication.   It tells you, when my words cannot, how I perceive something that is happening in my environment.

Parents, keep this in mind as well: persistent behavior may have an underlying medical cause. Food allergies and sensitivities, sleep disorders and gastrointestinal problems can all have profound effects on behavior.

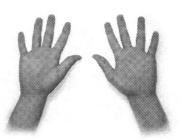

If you are a family member, please love me unconditionally.

Banish thoughts like, "If he would just—," and "Why can't she—." You did not fulfill every last expectation your parents had for you and you wouldn't like being constantly reminded of it. I did not choose to have autism. But remember that it is happening to me, not you. Without your support, my chances of successful, self-reliant adulthood are slim. With your support and guidance, the possibilities are broader than you might think. I promise you—I am worth it.

And finally, three words:
Patience. Patience. Patience.

Work to view my autism as a different ability rather than a disability. Look past what you may see as limitations and see the gifts autism has given me. It may be true that I'm not good at eye contact or conversation, but have you noticed that I don't lie, cheat at games, tattle on my classmates or pass judgment on other people? It's also true that I probably won't be the next Michael Jordan. But with my attention to fine detail and capacity for extraordinary focus, I might be the next Einstein. Or Mozart. Or Van Gogh.

They had autism, too.

The answer to Alzheimer's, the enigma of extraterrestrial life—what future achievements from today's children with autism, children like me, lie ahead?

All that I might become won't happen without you as my foundation. Think through some of those societal rules and if they don't make sense for me, let them go. Be my advocate, be my friend, and we'll see just how far I can go.

Chapter One

I am first and foremost a child. I have autism. I am not primarily "autistic."

Parents and professionals who operate within the autism community understand that when we use the word "autistic," we merely mean "of or relating to autism or a person with autism." But those of us who live with and love a child with autism also live with the frustrating lack of knowledge and unfair stereotypes assigned by the larger world. Whether we like it or not, "autistic" does not yet inspire general reactions of a favorable nature, does not yet stir the casual bystander to look beyond the label to see a whole person, splendidly full of both gifts and gaffs. The broader reaction, "Uh-oh. Silent, withdrawn head-banger," is still too common; the first assumption is one of limitations.

We change that perception one person at a time. And we begin by asking ourselves: what expectations do words set up?

No fan am I of gratuitous political correctness. That is not how I see "child first, with autism" vs. "autistic." I see it as an honest confrontation of how words can be accurate and yet set up expectations or preconceived notions that seriously impede progress toward attainable long-range goals.

The word "autistic" is accurate. But so are other words that we no longer use to describe people: spinster (unmarried woman), hobo (migrant worker), cripple (person with a physical handicap), and so on. The fact that a person is unmarried or has sustained a mobility-reducing injury or birth defect certainly figures into their life experiences, but it does not define their character—unless they or we let it.

Some people can use the word "autistic" purely as a descriptor, without attaching any limiting subconscious or preconceived notions to it. But if in stark and utter honesty with yourself, you come to see that shifting your perception of the word could benefit your child, remember that it's a process, not necessarily a lightening-bolt moment. It can take time and practice, even training, to do this. Ingrained views and experiences, how they affect the way we feel about and react to individuals with ASD, probably won't change overnight. Give yourself and others the time and latitude to accomplish this.

I personally abandoned the word "autistic" in describing my son almost immediately. What helped me out that door was a ridiculous website called www.hyperdictionary.com which pairs the word "autistic" with the synonym "unfit," and continues with a jaw-dropping list of 155 "related terms," including anesthetized, catatonic, emotionally dead, greedy, heartless, narcissistic, self-besot, soulless, unfeeling and untouchable. Not one of these words described my child—nor yours, I'll bet—so I worked up a list of my own "related terms" culled from the seven years of his K-5 experience: successful, involved, poised, hard-working, self-confident, unique, kind, polite, responsible and neat.

All that is autism is not in and of itself awful, although some components of it most certainly are, and some days will be infinitely more dreadful than others. But in the *long run*—and it is a long run—what you choose to believe about a child's autism may be the single biggest factor affecting his ultimate outcome. You are the possessor of a superpower: perspective. Consciously or otherwise, you make decisions based on your chosen perspective hundreds of times a day. Choosing to work towards changing an unproductive perspective is wildly courageous, empowering and doable.

Unconscious perspective is at work in our lives all the time. At least once in your life, haven't you paid lip service to the idea of not judging a book by its cover? It's a great piece of wisdom in theory, but in fact we judge people by our first impressions all the time.

Take that "fat person." Do we automatically put aside their obesity and think, "Wow! This person is fat—she/he must be awesome just like Winston Churchill, Luciano Pavarotti, Buddha, Babe Ruth!" Or do we react first to a *fat person*, possibly assigning uninformed misconceptions, such as, he must not have much self-control? "Myopics" are people who cannot succeed at certain activities without assistive technology—vision-correcting lenses. Without them, myopics cannot drive, read, play tennis, fly a plane or scuba dive. Hopefully, this is not our first thought when we meet a person in glasses. Helen Keller, Louis Braille, Ray Charles and Beethoven might have something to say about whether "impairment" limits achievement.

We all require some form of adaptation to our environment. Children with autism do require accommodation in order to achieve their fullest potential. Thank goodness we live in a time when the mysteries of autism are beginning to dissolve. We now know that modifications to curriculum, sensory and speech therapies and behavioral plans are tools that will lift our kids to achieve that which might otherwise be out of reach.

Losing sight of the whole child, losing him behind a label, makes your life more difficult, as well as his. Autism is not the cause of all of his foibles. All children spiral through equilibrium and disequilibrium as they cruise the developmental timeline. Most children will at some point test limits, potty-talk in public, elevate stubbornness to Olympic proportions, flush Batman down the toilet, neglect hygiene and cry when they don't get their way. Attributing it all to autism is not only inaccurate and unfair, but it robs you of experiencing the aspects of your child's development that are in fact typical! Again, all that is awful is not autism. He has hopes, preferences, likes, dislikes, fears and dreams just like any other child. In time (and with lots of communication therapy) he will be able to tell you about them, albeit maybe not with words.

So keep those channels wide open. Every child deserves to start his or her life and education with a slate clean of preconceived notions. Labels are not necessarily malicious but they are seldom harmless.

"Bryce is getting As in my classes," one of my son's teachers tells me at our first middle school parent conference. "He's an incredible student. He does everything that is asked of him, his homework is never late, he participates enthusiastically in class, and he is never off-task."

He goes on: "Bryce has exceeded everything I thought I knew about how much autistic kids can accomplish. I've had autistic kids in my classes. His creativity and organization are just far and above the others—"

His voice tapers off in mid-sentence. "I think I get it," he finally says. "That word, 'autistic,' sets up an expectation—

4

an expectation that is probably lower than what the child is capable of. Am I getting it?"

Yes, he "got it," and an already-good teacher "got" even better, for every child with autism who comes after Bryce. The teacher realized that every time he qualified "kid" with "autistic," it set a bar in his mind for what the child could or couldn't do. Everyone sets the bar at a different place, but it's dangerous business. Whether too low ("You don't think I can do it—why try?") or too high ("I'm never good enough —why try?"), should we force the child to travel the extra distance to meet what might be naive expectations? The road is long enough as it is.

So run the word "autistic" through your reality-checker and ask yourself if it in any way limits your view of what the future holds for your child or student with autism and the value he brings to your world. If it does, remember that nothing—*nothing*—is predetermined and that your time together is filled with open-ended opportunity.

Chapter Two

My sensory perceptions are disordered.

Sensory integration may be the most difficult aspect of autism to understand, but it is arguably the most critical. Cognitive and social learning cannot break through to a child whose world is intrusively loud, blindingly bright, unbearably malodorous and physically difficult to navigate. His brain cannot filter multiple inputs and he frequently feels overloaded, disoriented and unsettled in his own skin.

And into this shrieking, blinding hurricane of sensory acid rain we insert the expectation that this child "pay attention," "behave," learn, adhere to social rules which are mystifying to her, and communicate with us even though she has not the ability, the vocabulary and possibly not even the oral-motor capability. Neglect a child's sensory challenges and you will never even get close to discovering her capability. Sensory issues are *that* crucial to her overall ability to function.

Picture yourself on the world's grooviest roller coaster. (If you don't like roller coasters, this makes the example even better.) Coney Island and Six Flags are great vacation venues, but how long could you do your day job while ensconced on the Cyclone, the Xcelerator or the Millenium Force? Could you conduct that meeting, teach that class, be charming dinner company, write the report and clean the house while enduring the vertigo, the screams of fellow riders, the g-force of the rushing air, the unexpected drops and abrupt changes of direction, the sensation of hair in your mouth and bugs in your teeth? It might be fun as an occasional thrill but admit it—you are ready to get off after the three-minute ride. For many children with autism, there is no exit gate; it's a 24/7 affair and it is the very antithesis of thrilling.

It's natural that we shy away from things that are difficult to comprehend, that we look for an easier solution. There's no question that gaining a working understanding of sensory integration can, for the nonprofessional, be downright intimidating. It is an area of immense complexity; it pervades everything we do or try to do. And that is why it's the *first* outpost of autism we should address. It just sends me off the deep end when I hear sensory therapy described as an add-on, or something to "try" after everything else has been tried. Or that it's not real; it's "all in their heads."

It *is* all in their heads, all right. Research is beginning to actually see sensory dysfunction happening in the brain stem, great news for anyone who won't believe it until they see it. And actually, you may be looking right at it and simply not recognize the manifestation of sensory overload. Hands over the ears are obvious indications. Less obvious but no less compelling are the behaviors referred to as "stims," self-stimulating conduct such as rocking, chewing, flapping, rubbing, wandering and other repetitive mannerisms. Seemingly inexplicable behavior such as aggression, excessive silliness, clumsiness, over- or under-reaction to injury can all have an underlying sensory cause. In the case of more extreme behavior such as tantrums and meltdowns, the trigger may not be obvious at all; nevertheless, sensory overload should be the *first* suspect brought in for questioning. Even under harsh light, that questioning can be tricky, intricate and protracted. But one of the few universal truths about autism is this: no matter how unprovoked, how random it may appear, *behavior never, ever comes out of nowhere.* There is always a detonator (and we will discuss this at length in chapter nine). Find it you must, and keep in mind also that if your child is nonverbal or has limited verbal skills, she will not be able to tell you what is causing her such discomfort. Even your chatterbox Asperger's child, who seems so verbally competent, may not have vocabulary or awareness sophisticated enough to describe what is happening within her complicated neurology.

For the layperson, developing a working understanding of sensory integration can be challenging. But for most of us, even a little basic education will turn on the light bulb. Most of us are familiar with the basic five senses: visual (sight), auditory (sound), tactile (touch), olfactory (smell), and gustatory (taste). Less understood are the other two: vestibular (balance) and proprioceptive (position), and they can be wreaking untold and unimagined havoc in your child's life.

Comprehensive discussion of the sensory systems is beyond the scope of this chapter. An explosion of parent-friendly information has become available in just the last ten years, including many wonderful books and websites. I've listed just a couple of books at the end of the chapter to get you started; any occupational therapist will be able to recommend many more.

What follows here is "Sensory 101": a short description of each sense, and what its dysfunction can mean for the child with autism. An occupational therapist, an indispensable member of any child's autism team, can elaborate upon and address individual issues.

Note: Much of the discussion here centers on addressing hyper-acute sensory systems and how to calm overloaded senses. But it is also possible for senses to be hypo-acute, or under-responsive. The need in those cases is to alert, not calm, the under-responding sense. An occupational therapist can suggest alerting activities. We'll discuss hypo-acute responses in more detail in the next chapter. Bear in mind, too, that acuity may not be the same across all the child's senses. Some may be hyper, some may be hypo, and some can vary from day to day.

THE VISUAL SENSE

For many children with autism, the visual sense is their strongest. The good news/bad news is that while they rely more heavily upon visual input to learn and to navigate their world, it can be the first sense to become overstimulated. Bright lights or objects, reflective surfaces, too many objects in the field of vision or objects moving at fast or irregular speeds can all cause distortion and sensory chaos. So pervasive is this sense for so many children with autism that it warrants its own discussion later in the book.

THE AUDITORY SENSE

Our auditory sense provides us with a tremendous amount of information. We take in and instantly interpret not only the component qualities of sound—volume, pitch, frequency, vibration—but also the directionality of it. We turn our head to seek out voices, footsteps and traffic. If your hearing is typically calibrated, only the loudest sounds will cause you to recoil, cover your ears or otherwise protect yourself. For many individuals with autism, the auditory sense is the most frequently impaired. Hyper-acute hearing can cause real, agonizing pain. Hypo-acute hearing impacts language and social learning; what looks like laziness or noncompliance is in fact inability to filter and/or process ordinary, everyday sounds.

For the child with hyper-acute hearing, here it is in a nutshell: it's too loud, it's too high-pitched, it's too sudden and there are too many of them crowding in at once. And, not unlike a dog, the child with autism may actually hear things undetectable to your ear. Many children with autism lack the ability to suppress and/or filter sound, so the classroom or home setting that appears orderly to the casual observer is in fact a confusing minefield of clatter.

What it means for the child: Obvious "too loud" flags like blaring music, gymnasium basketball, cafeteria and playground cacophony, and emergency vehicle sirens are all examples of everyday commotion that can actually induce pain. Sudden loud sounds such as fire drills or cars backfiring can trigger a level of panic from which your child may take hours to recover. In extreme examples, the child has been able to hear the heartbeats of others in the room. As for enjoying the pounding surf at the beach—forget surf. Think "pounding," as in "headache."

Less apparent but just as invasive or intolerable are ordinary, seemingly non-threatening noises. He's not hiding in his room because he doesn't like his family; he's fleeing the dissonance of the dishwasher, coffeemaker, washer, dryer, television and teenager-on-the-cell-phone all having their say at once. He might as well be right inside that spin cycle himself. Over at school, the neuro-typical children in the classroom are listening to what the teacher is saying. But the child with autism cannot identify the voice of the teacher as the primary sound to which he should be attuned. To him it's indistinguishable from the grinding of the pencil sharpener, the fly buzzing on the windowsill, the lawn mower chugging outside, the child with the constant cough behind him and the class next door tromping down the hall to the library.

Well-known author Temple Grandin, who writes and speaks extensively about her own experiences as a person with autism, puts this succinct grace note on it: "Wal-Mart is like being inside the speaker at a rock and roll concert."

THE TACTILE SENSE

Tactile defensiveness is hypersensitivity to touch. Our skin registers an astonishing amount of information: light touches as well as deeper pressure, a wide range of temperatures, different types of pain or irritation, vibration and other movement, and textures ranging from slimy to rough. The child with autism is literally trapped in her own skin, unable to regulate unwanted sensations that rain upon her in the form of uncomfortable clothes, unwelcome touches from other people (hugs to you might be torture to her) and unpleasant textures of things she is confronted with touching or eating.

What it means to the child: Clothing tags, buttons, zippers, elastic around wrists or necks and similar clothing embellishments are a constant distraction. Whether indoors or out, going barefoot is not an option (do you have a tip-toe walker in your house?). The child may evade your embrace, and fight like a badger against haircuts, shampooing, teeth brushing, and nail clipping.

> Hands-on tasks like fingerpainting and sand table
> activities induce more stress than fun.

Some occupational therapists may tell you that tactile problems are among the most prevalent of all the sensory problems associated with autism. But most OTs will also tell you how successful they can be at desensitizing a hyperacute tactile sense. Take it from a mom whose child spent the early years of his life sporting only his birthday suit whenever he could get away with it and doling out "backwards" hugs to only a precious chosen few. By third grade he was in jeans and lovin' it. By fifth grade he was backpacking the great outdoors with all kinds of slimy-crawly critters and substances without batting an eye (as long as he and his Scoutmates could share contraband Skittles® in the tent each night). Patience, respect for the child's boundaries at each step, and a good occupational therapist will get you there.

THE OLFACTORY SENSE

"Ewwwww, what stinks?!" is a common refrain in our household, even when my nose detects nothing. Paraeducators have told me that their students with autism may greet them with "You smell funny!" even when they are fresh from the shower. Olfactory defensiveness—hyperacute sense of smell—is common among children with autism.

> **What it means for the child:** Aromas, scents and
> fragrances regarded by the typical population as
> pleasant or even undetectable have the power to
> make the child with autism miserable, even ill. If a
> certain paint, glue, perfume or floor cleaner has
> ever given you an instant headache, if the smell of

fish, broccoli, garlic, cat food or limburger cheese has ever turned your stomach or brought tears to your eyes, multiply that sensation many times over and you'll get some idea of what your child may be coping with. Please don't ask your child to change the kitty litter box—that "odor free"/natural citrus/recycled pine concoction, combined with the you-know-what that lurks within, will probably knock the poor kid back into yesterday.

Some years ago, my son's olfactory issues nearly derailed a long anticipated trip to Disneyland when it had barely begun. It was his first airplane trip, and in an effort to keep everything as familiar as possible, we had booked a rental car of the same make and model as our car at home. I told Bryce that a car "like ours" would be waiting at the end of our plane trip to take us to the hotel. Having (still!) vastly underestimated his literal thinking, I realized too late that he was picturing our very own car coming out of the cargo hold in Los Angeles along with our luggage. The rental was "like ours," but with a horrible twist—it was new. Now, for many people, that "new car smell" ranks right up there with cinnamon buns and baby powder as a favorite. But for Bryce, it was a show-stopper. "This is a SMELLY car!" he decreed. "A SMELLY, SMELLY CAR!!!" It took an eternity to get him into the car, and another eternity of listening to the "SMELLY CAR!!" mantra all the way into town. Do I need to tell you we took the hotel shuttle to the park the next day?

Here are a Dirty Dozen of possible olfactory offenders in the home: scented laundry products (remember that if it's on his clothes, he cannot get away from it!), scented soaps and shampoos (even "kid" scents, such as bubble gum, can offend), bathroom air "fresheners" (they only add another layer of odor), hand lotions, deodorants, aftershaves, body gels, hair products, house-cleaning products such as ammonia, bleach, other fragranced cleaners, cooking odors like fish or broccoli, yard and garden chemicals.

In the school setting we have the paint area, odiferous science projects, the classmate wearing cologne, the old oil-burning furnace or the window that opens onto the newly-mowed, composting lawn, the hamster cage and the days-old forgotten lunch in the closet. More than one student with autism has been known to experience the uncontrollable gag reflex in the cafeteria. Offer an alternative place to eat lunch if lunchtime smells are unpleasant.

> *Did you hear the one about the little boy who went camping for the first time? Standing outside his tent amid a beautiful pine forest, he wailed, "I hate it here! It smells like floor cleaner!"*

THE GUSTATORY SENSE

The gustatory sense is our sense of taste, and it is closely tied to the olfactory sense. The olfactory sense acts as a kind of sentry: if a potential food item smells dangerous—moldy, burnt, rancid or otherwise "off"—we don't put it in our mouths. It's nature's way of protecting us from ingesting poisons and toxins.

A hyper-acute gustatory system reacts with increased sensitivity to pungent tastes like bitterness (such as the phytochemicals found in many vegetables) and "heat" (spicy foods containing capsaicin, such as chili). It may also reject foods based on temperature or texture: the child may shun very cold foods (ice cream or refrigerated juice), oozy/slippery foods (puddings, canned peaches, condiments) or foods that are a mix of textures, such as casseroles, sand-wiches or soups. The grainy texture of meat frequently offends, as may carbonated drinks (this is actually a plus, isn't it?).

On the other end of the sensitivity scale is the hypo-taster. This child may have a reduced perception of taste, and may do one of three things: 1) eat everything in sight because to them it all tastes good, 2) eat not much at all because food as a pleasant sensory experience has no mean-ing or interest, or 3) eat a horrifying array of nonfood items as they seek the sensory input they are not getting, like dirt, clay, glue, coffee grounds, dust bunnies and paper.

What this means to the child: Many children with ASD are "picky eaters" to a breathtaking degree. Their extremely limited palettes—often as few as two foods will be acceptable to a child—may be a result of hyper- or hypo-acute olfactory and/or gustatory functions.

The health implications for both supertasters and hypo-tasters are potentially troubling. The hyper-tasters reject many of the foods providing the highest health benefits, like vegetables. The hypo-tasters are susceptible to just the opposite, the excesses of oral gratification and illnesses associated with overeating and, later in their adult life, alco-hol and smoking.

Addressing gustatory sensitivities requires time and patience. For the sake of your own sanity, "don't try this at home" without the aid of an occupational therapist.

THE VESTIBULAR AND PROPRIOCEPTIVE SENSES

These two critical senses can be very difficult for parents and laypersons to understand. Like a well-run corporate accounting office, they get no attention when everything is running smoothly. It is only when things go awry that we become aware of the mayhem that is created when an essential piece of infrastructure is malfunctioning.

The *vestibular system* regulates the sense of equilibrium (balance, stability) by responding to changes in the position of the eyes and head. Its "command center" is located in the inner ear. The *proprioceptive sense* uses feedback from joints and muscles to tell us where our body is in space and what forces and pressures are acting upon it.

What it means to the child: Impairments to the vestibular and proprioceptive senses can greatly hamper or even halt everyday motor functions. Children with such difficulties may literally trip over their own feet, bounce off walls and fall out of chairs. They may experience *gravitational insecurity*, becoming anxious in any setting that takes their feet off solid ground, such as climbing the steps to the slide, using a public toilet, riding a bike and sitting on a too-tall chair or stool without a footrest. Anxieties about managing their fundamental movements can be magnified by the additional expectation that they learn new skills, whether cognitive/academic, social or gross motor. In this regard, it's not hard to understand why many ASD children shy away from sports, with its overwhelming multiple expectations: assume certain positions, listen for instructions, learn and perform one or more gross motor skills, remember the rules, *understand* the rules and communicate with your teammates (get yelled at by teammates and adults when you blow a play).

And because vestibular and proprioceptive problems are not easily recognized by the untrained eye, the danger is that they go unidentified and untreated, leaving the child with autism to cope unaided with a very hostile environment.

Vestibular disorder can affect nearly every function of the body, causing a dizzying (no pun intended!) range of symptoms including but not limited to: loss of balance, chronic nausea, distorted hearing (ears may feel "stuffed" or sound may come across as full of static, like bad radio reception), visual disturbances (objects or print material appears to be blurry or in motion, distance focus is difficult, glare from lights exaggerated), difficulty with memory and/or focus, chronic fatigue, acute anxiety and depression.

Children with proprioceptive difficulties may walk with an odd, heavy gait, have trouble with tableware, pencils and other fine motor implements, lose their balance when their eyes are closed, or be "crashers," forever running into or jumping off things as they seek deep pressure sensory input.

In addition to that indispensable occupational therapist, an adapted PE specialist can help with large motor issues, modifying curriculum and equipment so your child can participate with his peers in PE and playground activities. Ask your school district's special education motor team.

One of the occupational therapist's most effective tools is a child-specific plan of action called the sensory diet, sometimes also called a sensory map. A sensory diet identifies a child's particular sensory needs and prescribes regularly scheduled activities that help him organize sensory input in a manner that makes it easier for him to engage, attend and self-regulate. Through formal and informal observation and evaluation, your OT will determine three main components:

- The child's level of sensory arousal throughout the day. Low arousal/hypo-sensitivity requires alerting inputs. Over-arousal/hyper-sensitivity requires calming inputs.

- Current state of the child's sensory systems (which senses are strengthened and which are challenged).

- Documentation of specific incidents that set off emotional or behavioral responses (transitions, certain activities, locations or people, having to deal with certain substances).

This information illuminates where to focus, and a plan is developed accordingly. The OT will break the child's day down into defined segments and lay out activities for each. Such activities might include regularly scheduled movement breaks, providing fidget or chew toys, and providing a study carrel or "quiet corner." Embedding into his day those activities that both address his needs and play to his strengths will give him a sense of control and can-do that greatly enhances his ability to engage both cognitively and socially.

Forget the Pyramid of Giza and the Hanging Gardens of Babylon, the real Seven Wonders of the World are the neurological senses whose function or dysfunction hold such profound power over us. Seven years of devoted sensory training took my wordless, aggressive toddler and helped turn him into the confident and kind-hearted scholar, artist, athlete and fun teen he is today. Now that's a monument.

Suggested reading:

Building Bridges Through Sensory Integration by Ellen Yack, Paula Aquilla, Shirley Sutton

The Out-of-Sync Child and *The Out-of-Sync Child Has Fun*, both by Carol Kranowitz

Sensory Smarts: A Book for Kids with ADHD or ASD Struggling with Sensory Integration Problems by Kathleen Chara

Raising a Sensory Smart Child: The Definitive Handbook for Helping Your Child with SI Issues by Lindsey Biel

Smart Moves: Why Learning Is Not All in Your Head by Carla Hannaford, Ph.D.

Chapter Three

Please remember to distinguish between won't (I choose not to) and can't (I am not able to).

Is a zebra white with black stripes or black with white stripes? Ask ten people or look at ten websites and you'll get twelve opinions. Zebras give the impression of being white with black stripes because the stripes end before joining under the belly and around the legs. But the hide of the zebra is actually black. It's a lesson from Mother Nature that things are not always as they appear on the surface.

And so it is with many of the complexities of autism. How do we distinguish between what our child *won't do* (chooses not to) and what he *can't do* (is not able to)? Many "won't" allegations about our kids are behavior complaints: He just won't comply; she won't listen to instructions; he won't stop rapping his knuckles, walking away in mid-sentence or other odd, inexplicable or narrowly focused actions. "Won't" and "can't" are not interchangeable. "Won't," the contracted form of "will not," implies that his noncompliance is deliberate. "Can't," the contracted form of "can not," acknowledges that noncompliance is not a matter of choice, but attributable to lack of ability, knowledge or opportunity.

Understanding the distinction between "can't" and "won't" is actually simple, because where behavior is concerned, there are two absolutes:

- All behavior is communication.

- All behavior happens for a reason.

Today's psychology generally recognizes six reasons/ motivations for behavior. The next time you catch yourself saying, "He just won't—," stop and evaluate your child's behavior in light of the following. See if some of the "I choose not to" starts fading into "I am not able to."

1. Resistant/avoidant—you are asking your child or student to do something he doesn't know how to do or is unpleasant to him for a reason that you do not perceive.

It is natural for any child to want to evade an unpleasant task. Pinpointing the source of the resistance is the name of the game. Your essential role is now behavior detective. You may be surprised at how often lack of ability, information or opportunity plays into noncompliance or nonperformance: think "close to 100% of the time." Possible reasons (get some coffee; we are going to be here a while): he doesn't comprehend the instructions/the request, doesn't know or understand the rules/process/routine, doesn't have the fine or gross motor skills to accomplish the task, the behavioral or academic expectation is too high, the activity is sensory-overwhelming, the task causes physical discomfort or the request comes at a time when he is hungry or too tired to comply. In order words—he can't.

On top of that, he almost certainly dreads failure and the resulting criticism. His world is one of concrete, black-and-white, all-or-nothing perspective. Errors and successes come in two sizes: huge or nonexistent. The stress and anxiety this produces in him is pervasive. Further, is he offered any choice or flexibility in how and/or when the task is accomplished? Has he any say in how he could best tackle it?

Avoidance behaviors frequently stem from lack of comprehension and fear of failure. Experiencing success motivates willingness to work, to try, even to strive.

2. Attention-seeking—your child wants adult or peer attention.

The good news is—he wants to interact! The bad news is that inappropriate attention-seeking behavior frequently disrupts classrooms and family routine. If you are exasperated because he "won't" stop, get out the deerstalker again and consider: does he know how to ask for attention/help in an appropriate manner? It's one of autism's nasty Catch 22s that the child needs to be carefully taught about social interaction, but at the same time lacks the understanding of when and how to ask for what he needs. He will need specific instruction and examples (not to mention needing to summon the courage) to make requests such as "I need help" or "I don't understand this." While teaching him to ask for attention appropriately, also consider whether he is simply not getting sufficient adult attention to achieve what's expected of him. Similarly, is he getting adequate and appropriate attention from peers to validate his self-worth? Does he get more attention from you for his undesirable deeds than he does for the more suitable behaviors? Is the amount of praise he hears from you equal to or greater than the amount of complaining?

Here is the trickier step: watch what you reinforce. If you ignore her when she's not being disruptive but take immediate notice when the spitballs start sailing or the sofa is being used as a trampoline, well, she's gotten the attention she wanted, and you've succeeded in reinforcing her inappropriate behaviors. Action—reaction. Remember our maxim: all behavior is communication. It applies to you, too.

3. Self-regulation—your child is attempting to calm or alert over- or under-stimulated senses, thereby reducing anxiety or discomfort. This may be the underlying organic cause of a behavior.

In chapter two we discussed sensory disorder, focusing largely on hypersensitive responses and how they interfere with your child's ability to attend and learn, to self-control behavior and be socially engaged. Where persistent or unusual behavior is present, it can be just as important to consider that your child may be attempting to self-regulate hyposensitivity, that is, to alert or stimulate under-responsive senses. A few examples:

- Under-stimulated visual sense: child sways or rocks (attempting to change angle of visual perspective), is leery of changes in elevation (ladders, stairs) or is fascinated with moving objects (model trains, water wheels).

- Under-stimulated auditory sense: child speaks too loudly, likes noisy appliances (lawn mowers, hair dryers, blenders), handles toys, books and other objects roughly so as to create crashing noises, is fascinated with rushing water (waterfalls, running bathwater, flushing toilets) or likes vibrating/buzzing toys.

- Under-stimulated tactile sense: child may "stim" to the point of hurting himself (biting, pinching, applying pressure with various objects) and then seemingly not notice (high threshold to pain and cold). He may purposely bump into objects and other people or may prefer tight, heavy or textured clothing.

- Under-stimulated olfactory sense: child may seem over-interested in smelling or sniffing his own body and others. She may eat unusual nonfood items such as dirt, paste, coins or soap, or she may exhibit lack of sensitivity to odors other consider offensive, such as urine (bedwetting) and feces (smearing). Note: both of the foregoing can also be signs of an understimulated tactile sense.

- Under-stimulated gustatory sense: child may eat either everything in sight or virtually nothing, may eat nonfood items, or may eat unusual taste combinations of food (e.g. pickles and ice cream, French fries dipped in peach yogurt, peanut butter on his hot dog).

4. Entertainment/fun—the child finds a particular behavior amusing to himself or others.

Children with ASD often have a more rigid or reduced sense of play than typical kids, but they can also be very resourceful at entertaining themselves. It's actually an awesome skill, as any mother of an "I'm bored—what can I do?" kid will tell you. If the diverting behavior is one that your child repeats even when others are not present, it may be his way of telling you he wants to play but has neither adequate skill nor the opportunity to interact with other children. The door is open, Coach. Set up a game plan.

5. Control—child is attempting to order or reorder his environment.

When so little is within their control, many children with ASD experience life as a continuous battle to hold onto whatever power they do have to direct their lives. Their attempts to control may be overt (confrontational, aggressive behavior that looks like defiance), or they may be passive-aggressive (they silently or covertly continue to do what they wish to do regardless of attempts at redirecting behavior).

Your daily life as a typical adult is a perpetual, minute-by-minute stream of choices. You take for granted all the choices you have, and even more importantly, the fact that you are able to make choices. It is an ability requiring reasoning and decision-making skills that are much more limited in your child with autism.

The good news is that what appears to be controlling behavior on your child's part can also be seen as evidence of her ability to think independently and affirm her own wants and needs. Channel these qualities as you work with her to instill decision-making skills and increase the number of choices and opportunities for success in her world.

It's all-too-easy to get into a power struggle with a child who seems hell-bent on having things his way, but always remind yourself of your goals for this child before you respond. Is your goal to bend the child to your will, make him respect your authority and force his compliance, at all costs? (Ask yourself, is that really a "win" for either of you?) Or is the goal to gradually acclimate him to socially acceptable behavior in a manner that makes it possible for him to grow as a person and take his place as a citizen of the world? As a young child, Bryce had a very definite passive-aggressive manner of letting us know when he had had enough of a social situation: he would tell us—once. If we did not move to end the outing within a reasonable timeframe (measured in less than five minutes), he would simply turn and go.

Depending upon where we were, you can only imagine how dangerous this could be. I still break out in hives just remembering some of those times, his little back disappearing down the street or into the crowd. We quickly learned that when Bryce was ready to go, it was nonnegotiable, *arrivederci* time. Was he "pulling our strings"? Were we "letting him run the show"? Not by a long shot. He was simply telling us that he had reached his meltdown point. We respected that, ungrudgingly, and adapted our plans accordingly. Our goal was for Bryce to be able to handle social settings in a manner that would allow us to do things as an entire family. In order to accomplish that goal, we had to learn to listen and heed his verbal warnings when he had reached the limits of his current abilities. We did indeed make numerous hasty retreats in those days, but over time Bryce made huge gains in language, confidence, sensory tolerance, and social skills. We did it his way and today, we have a practically go-anywhere kid.

6. Retribution—child wants to retaliate for treatment perceived as unfair.

I include this one here only because it is most likely a motivation you can rule out.

"He's only doing it to get back at me." Let it go, my friend. The concept of fair/unfair requires the ability to perceive or imply the motivations and feelings of others, something children with autism are notoriously lacking. What's more, planning and carrying out revenge is an advanced executive skill coupled with a level of motor planning well beyond the abilities of most children on the spectrum. Keep looking. Your answer isn't here.

About-face!

But "can't" is a two-faced monster. "Can't" comes in two flavors, and it sits on a very different place on the tongue when "can't" is coming from you rather than your child. You, as the capable adult in this equation, do not get off the hook with "can't." "Can't," as we have defined it, is about lack of knowledge, ability and opportunity. It is not about backing away from difficulty and challenge. You didn't get a choice about the nature part of your whole child, but you certainly have all due influence in the nurture part. To a great degree, your child will be a reflection of his environment. What vibe does he get from you? Are you a "can-do" adult?

A Tale of Two Fathers

"I simply *can't* handle the day-to-dayness of it."

I met this father at the very first autism support group meeting I ever attended. He was referring to the meltdowns, the nonresponsiveness, the "stims," and the food peculiarities: "My wife is much better at that than me. I am focusing on providing financially for the family and realizing that I must do so for this child, most probably, lifelong. I'm working on setting that up." My immediate reaction was that his wife was gonna be mighty tired, probably permanently. But I was at the beginning of the process myself. Later I understood and gave him all due credit for the fact that he was willingly and unflinchingly owning up to his limitations and was trying to build constructive compensation. He was hewing a learning path not so very different from that of autism itself. He was learning that his plans and goals as a parent were going to be different than he originally envisioned them; not bad—just different. He was not in denial. He was in the midst of his own grieving process and working through it. Because of that, there was every possibility that with time, he could and would acclimate to his atypical child, that this dad's "can't handle it" attitude could change to "can and will," and that he would achieve that greater connection which could make a critical difference in his son's life.

Contrast him with another dad I met through a friend, a dad stuck like a broken record on an anti-government rant about how, by mandating vaccines for school attendance, he had been robbed of his son: "I simply *cannot* relate to him. How do you think it feels to know that he'll probably end up in jail?" Well, it's almost certainly a scary, helpless feeling weighed down further by regrets and broken dreams. But it crosses the line from *can't* (am not able to) into *won't* (I choose not to) with the decision to look only backward into what-might-have-been, rather than forward into possibilities yet unexplored. Regardless of whether a vaccination is actually liable for his son's condition—and I will not debate that subject in this book—it is still an after-the-fact discussion. The child *cannot* (proper use of the word here) be un-vaccinated. By adopting a defeatist attitude rather than the more difficult, work-intensive proactive approach, this dad also chose paralysis, fear, exasperation and self-fulfilling prophecy. His son is eight years old. He is clearly a bright, articulate, clever and resourceful child. He is also aggressive, angry and frustrated—like Dad. Through a lifetime of quasi-subliminal messages, "can't" can plant the germ of despair in a child.

I suggest to this father: try to reframe your "can't." Your son can't change that he has autism. He can't find his way to something better if the adults around him are unwilling to help. Remember that "can't" means "am not able to," and unless you step up to the plate, your child's life will be filled with legitimate can'ts. For you, "can't" can be a four-letter word. For you, "can't" is a choice, one of many choices you are free to make, and your child isn't.

I told this father: I happen to know you are more capable than that. And I asked him, as my pediatrician used to ask me, a question that is sometimes difficult to face down: Who is the adult here? Who has the power to change things?

The irony and the tragedy of can't vs. won't is that we adults often kill the very thing we want most dearly to achieve. If you yearn for a child who is confident, optimistic, curious and engaged, that is what you must model and that is what you must find every little instance of and reinforce in him, however tiny the increment of gain. Think very carefully about the role of reinforcement in your relationship with your child or student. The nuances may be subtle, but the bottom line is this: the manner in which you respond to your child's actions, words or attitude amounts to an endorsement. Watch what you reinforce; be absolutely sure it is something you want him or her to repeat. When you take on a can-do attitude, he can-do, too.

If you find yourself governed by thoughts such as, I can't give this child special treatment, I can't put extra time into modifying assignments or environments, and I can't do anything about the way this kid is, then you can't expect to see any positive changes. Thoughtfully constructing the child's world in a manner that ensures a flow of successes, however bite-sized they may be, builds a foundation that buries the won'ts beneath it. That's not special treatment. It's what we like to think of as "the right way."

Think back to those pre-Cambrian days before you had a child: if you went to a bar after work, they called it "Happy Hour" or maybe "Attitude-Adjustment Hour." This isn't that much different—you choose to make a conscious shift in your mental state. If you don't like the boozy connotation, think of it as energy resource management: how much time and energy do you expend dwelling on what you don't have and can't have? That's called brooding. How much could you accomplish if you redirected that energy into doing, trying and reaching forward? That's called progress.

Chapter Four

I am a concrete thinker. This means I interpret language very literally.

Whatever command of your native language you thought you had will be seriously tested by your literal minded child or student with autism. You will be "taken at your word" in a manner you never had to confront before. In the column I write for *Autism Asperger's Digest*, I described the pitfalls of colloquial communication, beginning with this woeful assertion from British Olympic medalist Doug Larson: "If the English language made any sense, a catastrophe would be an apostrophe with fur."

To children with autism, with their concrete, visual thinking, their (often brilliant) associative abilities and, for many, their limited vocabularies, the imagery generated by some of our most common idioms and other figures of speech must be very disturbing. Ants in his pants? Butterflies in her stomach? Open a can of worms? Cat got your tongue?

It's enough to make them want to drive the porcelain bus. (Like that one? It means throw up—er—vomit.)

Actually, that very imagery they conjure up is at the root of some of our everyday expressions. When you tell him it's raining cats and dogs, what you really mean is that it's raining very hard. One interpretation of the origin of this idiom (there are many) goes back several hundred years to the English floods of the 17th and 18th centuries. After torrential downpours, the streets would be littered with the bodies of cats and dogs that had drowned in the storm. It looked as if they had rained from the skies.

And I am sure this is what a lot of young ones with autism visualize when you say it's raining cats and dogs. ("I don't see them!" fretted one little boy. "It only looks like falling-down water!") Heaven help you if he hears you telling someone it's a dog-eat-dog world, that you toasted the bride and groom at the reception, or that you warned someone not to throw the baby out with the bathwater.

You wouldn't dream of knowingly issuing instructions to your child in a foreign language, but English can seem that way. A popular Internet essay notes: "There is no egg in egg-plant, neither apple nor pine in pineapple. A guinea pig is neither from Guinea nor is it a pig. If the plural of tooth is teeth, why isn't the plural of booth beeth? One goose, two geese. So one moose, two meese? If teachers taught, why haven't preachers praught? We have noses that run and feet that smell. How can a slim chance and a fat chance be the same, while a wise man and a wise guy are opposites?"

The lunacy continues with homographs: The nurse wound gauze around the wound. Farms produce produce. The birds scattered, and the dove dove into the woods. When you get close to the window, close it. Lead me to the lead pipe. Go polish the Polish table. Can you wind your watch in the wind?

The bottom line is that communicating with a child with autism is astonishingly easier when we pause to consider our words. It may take a bit of retraining—yours, not his.

Here are some common snags to watch for:

Idioms and clichés:

Don't say	Instead say
You are the apple of my eye.	I love you very much.
I'm at the end of my rope.	I'm about to get angry.
Bite your tongue!	Please don't speak to me like that.
Let's call it a day.	It's time to stop for now.
I smell a rat.	This doesn't seem right to me.

Nonspecific instructions

It's important to *say exactly what you mean* and don't make your child or student figure out nonspecific instructions.

Don't say	Instead say
Hang it over there.	Hang your coat on the hook by the door.
Stay out of the street.	Stop your bike at the end of the driveway.
Quit kicking.	Keep your feet under your desk.
Let's get going.	We are going home now.

Inferences

Similar to the nonspecific instruction, an inference comes across to the child with autism as merely a statement of fact. Don't make him guess. Specify the action you want him to take.

Don't say	Instead say
Your room's a mess!	Please hang up your clothes.
You didn't turn your homework in.	Please put your book report on my desk.
It's too cold outside for that.	Wear long pants instead of shorts today.
I don't like that noise.	Please turn down the sound on the TV.

Phrasal Verbs

Phrasal verbs combine a verb with a preposition or adverb to form common expressions that can be just as confusing as idioms to the concrete thinker.

Don't say	Instead say
We look up to him.	We admire him; he sets a good example.
The car is acting up.	The car (or part of the car) is not working right.
Jamie was kicked out of class.	Jamie was sent to talk with the principal.
Let's wrap this up.	It's time to stop playing trains.

By now you are getting an inkling of how much of our everyday conversation is imprecise and, to the ASD child, illogical. You'll learn even more quickly the first time you tell him to "wait just a minute for me" and he is not there when you come back in five. "Gone in sixty seconds" will take on a whole new meaning beyond the time involved in boosting a locked car. Um—I mean—*stealing* a locked car.

And while we are on the subject of sloppy talk, expecting a child with autism to follow teenage conversation is ludicrous. "We was talking and stuff, and I'm, like, I am SO not going there! And he just went, okay whatever, and I'm like FINE! Like I could care less, and then he goes, like, yeah bite me—" Parents and teachers! It is *more* than okay to require siblings and classmates to speak comprehensible English around individuals with autism. If you had to translate the foregoing passage, it would be something like: "I didn't want to talk with Duane anymore. We were both starting to say things that were unkind." Remember the scene in that irreverent old movie *Airplane*? "Pardon me, Stewardess, I speak jive." If different forms of our own native English (black, southern, Cockney, Boston, Irish) can be confusing to you, just think of what a Tower of Babel they are to the child with autism.

To have a child who struggled with language was the ultimate irony for me. My college diploma says "B.S., Speech Communication" on it. Somewhere in my garage is a crate full of gently rusting debate trophies from high school. Yes, I am a certified windbag. I come from a family of inveterate punsters and wordmeisters, forever dreaming up obscure word games. It took a major learning curve on my part to, first, realize my child wasn't capable of or even interested in this kind of verbal jousting, and second, to accept that if I wanted to communicate meaningfully with him (and oh, how I did!), I would have to rework my own manner of presentation. I had to actually think before I spoke. Shouldn't we all? This is one of the gifts autism gave me. I had to carefully choose my words, my tone of voice, my inflection. If I didn't, he would tune me out, without malice, without annoyance and without the slightest indication that I was even in the room.

And you thought this didn't happen until the teen years.

Actually, getting into the practice of communicating with your child on his custom wavelength is excellent preparation for the teen years. Start listening now to everything your child wants to tell you, including that which is not verbal. Look at him when he speaks to you, and answer him every time he speaks to you. (Non-response from him tells you: message undeliverable! Try a different way.) Setting up that reciprocal exchange (he hears you, you hear him) gives him confidence in the value of his message, whatever it may be. That confidence will become the motivation that eventually moves him beyond concrete responses to spontaneous offerings, and finally, initiating thoughtful and thought-filled conversation. That's a day all parents and teachers of language-challenged children yearn for and dream about.

While you are working on framing your communication in more concrete terms, be assured your child will give you lots of gentle, judgment-free direction to keep you on track. Most of our family was tickled to death when Bryce reached the point of being able to handle answering the phone. My mother, a health professional with a great understanding of neurological disorders, nonetheless tripped herself up nearly every time she called. "Hi, Bryce!" she'd say. "What are you doing?" To which he would reply, *every time*: "Well,

Grandma, I'm talking to you on the phone." We all learned to ask better, more concrete questions, the kind that actually lead to conversation: What did you do in science class today? What would you like to do that's fun this weekend? Are you reading a good book this week?

My most infamous idiom tale happened when Bryce was about seven, and I call it "The Terrible Weary Battle of the Hangnail." It was one of those incidents that escalate inexorably from nothing to warfare before you have time to realize what's happening.

He came to me with a tiny hangnail on the index finger. No big deal, I said, I'll just nip it off with the nail clippers.

"Nooooooooooo!" he shrieked, with gale force. "It will HURT!"

This child had spent his whole life being impervious to true pain and extreme cold. But all of a sudden, and for reasons I could not imagine, this hangnail was an antagonist of Goliath proportions.

First, the usual rebuttals. It won't hurt. I promise. I'll be very quick. Look the other way. No? Okay, you can do it yourself. No clippers? Just bite it off. No. We'll numb it with an ice pack first. No. We'll soften it up with a warm bath. No.

Out came plans B, C, D, E, F and G, like some horrid *Cat in the Hat* variation. All were rejected. Exasperation on both sides escalated sharply.

The evening wore on. Was that me, almost shouting? I knew I was losing it, being sucked in, sucked down, seemingly unable to break the fall. Now two people were miserable instead of one.

"Look," I said. "Here are the choices: I nip it off. You nip it off. Or you just live with it."

"Nooooooooooooo!"

Envision the scarlet face, tears flying, and hair matted with sweat.

Bedtime finally came, and with it, a mom with the determination of Houdini. As I bent to tuck him in, so stealthily palming the nail clipper, I grabbed his finger and the hangnail was history. The pure surprise on his face was unforgettable.

"There," I said. "Did it hurt?"

"No."

The next morning I took him up on my lap and told him two things. First, he had to trust me. If I tell him something will not hurt, I mean it. I would always be honest with him if something was going to hurt, like a shot. I respected his preference for the truth, however unpleasant. So when I say it's not going to hurt, it's not going to hurt.

But just as importantly, I told him, I really admired his tenacity. I explained that "tenacity" meant that he really stood by what he believed, didn't back down, resisted pressure. That took strength and determination. "You really stuck to your guns," I said, "and that can be a very good thing." The words hadn't even cleared my lips before I knew I had goofed. A dark cloud instantly eclipsed a troubled face.

"I don't want to stick to a gun!" he cried, truly alarmed.

And then:

"Are you sure you didn't mean—*gum*?"

Chapter Five

Please be patient with my limited vocabulary.

"You can't rush art."

Bryce was seven years old when he turned his bottomless blue eyes on his first grade teacher and delivered this zinger. It was hustle time as she prodded the class to clean up their paints: "Quick-quick-quick! It's time for music! Brushes in the sink! Line up at the door! Let's go!" Bryce had just discovered the wonder of mixing orange and green paint to make brown for his version of *Sunflowers*, and he had his own opinion about all the hurry-scurry. His teacher couldn't wait to tell me about his remark because "of course, he is right."

What she didn't know was that he lifted the response, lock, stock and barrel (words, inflection and tempo), right out of *Toy Story 2*. Bryce had a breathtaking command of delayed echolalia. When his own limited vocabulary failed him, he had split-second retrieval of entirely functional responses from the encyclopedic stash of movie scripts stored on the hard drive of his very own brain.

Echolalia is a verbal behavior common in autism where the child repeats chunks of language that he has heard uttered by others. It can be *immediate* (child echoes something that has just been said to or near him), *delayed* (child repeats something he heard in recent, mid- or distant past) or *perseverative* (child repeats the same phrase or question over and over again).

There's a piercing sense of panic that foments in parents when the exchange of fact, feeling and thought cannot flow freely between themselves, their child and the rest of the world.

At the time of the "can't rush art" incident, about 90% of Bryce's speech was delayed-echolalic. Even though he was so skillful at it that it was largely undetectable to anyone but our family, I was still desperate, *desperate* to squash it. This is a very common but somewhat misguided desire for parents in my position. It's understandable, because—as long as we are quoting movies—it can look like "what we've got here is a failure to communicate." It can seem that way because the speech is not spontaneous. And with many kids, it doesn't seem to have any relevance to what's happening at the moment, although to the child, it does. He may be three or four associative links out ahead of you, making it a tricky but necessary job to discover the correlation.

I have felt with a mother's heart, as you may be feeling, the urgency to have your child produce "normal" speech, the kind that erases some of the stark difference between him and his age peers. But in that urgency, we must not lose sight of this: having a means of functional communication, *whatever it may be*, is what's truly essential, to any child, but even more so to the child with autism. If you take away only one thing from this chapter, let it be this: while she is struggling for basic vocabulary and for the skills involved with "normal" generative speech, she still needs a way to communicate her needs, fears and wants. Indeed, if she cannot get those needs met and fears quelled, her world and yours can be a horrid place. Without functional communication, *in whatever form it may take*, expect to see her frustration and fear play out in behavior, as she tries to let you know by any means possible, that things are not as they should be for her. But once she is comfortable that she can communicate and that *you are listening* regardless of her mode of communication, she can actively begin to build an understanding of all facets of communication, including the ones that go beyond mere vocabulary:

- Nonverbal forms of communicating (gestures, actions, facial expressions, body language, art media, music) can convey meaning and/or emphasis, either unintentionally or when words fail us.

- People are more than just vessels for imparting information, and conversation is more than just a means of getting needs satisfied. Initiating language (intentionally engaging other people) opens the door to experiences that can be pleasant, interesting, and even comforting.

Language is so much more than just being able to slap a label on items, feelings or actions! Language in all its vivid, wonderful and infuriating complexity is pervasive—it is everywhere at all times and it is not something learned in a speech therapist's office thirty minutes a week. Echolalia is only one aspect of language development, albeit it is a common one that generates a lot of emotion in parents. We want it *gone.* Hang on (for dear life) to that speech therapist, who will advise you about equally important language issues such as oral/motor problems (difficulty with the actual musculature of the mouth, tongue, face and throat) and different teaching methods. But know also that immersing your child in an ongoing language-rich environment is the surest way to build vocabulary and understanding of the intricacies of spoken communication. Nearly all children, including neuro-typical ones, learn language through imitation: "Say 'mama'! Say 'doggie'!" Your child's penchant for echolalia proves his proficiency at absorbing language imitatively. Use it, by providing meaningful language outlets at every opportunity. This is why books (in print or on CD) are exponentially superior to video games, why the television should not be allowed to override dinner conversation and why you should read to your children until they boot you forcibly from their rooms (mine were in middle school when this happened, and they actually were very polite about it). In particular, if your child is in a self-contained special education classroom, she may not have much exposure to typically-developing "kidspeak." Seek those opportunities for her outside the classroom.

But back to echolalia. Fortunately for me (and for Bryce, so he didn't have to grow up with a half-demented mother), two things happened concurrently that eased my mind enough that I could back off and let him work through his echolalia in his own way and at his own pace. The first was an article I read in *The Advocate*, the Autism Society of America's publication. It was written by a young man with autism, twenty years old, very successfully making his way through a four-year college. He was very frank about the fact that he still employed echolalia in his ordinary social communication, and that he alone knew it. I thought, *Huh!* Maybe all the stress I'm heaping on this isn't quite warranted.

The second thing that happened was that I finally called in an autism specialist to discuss it. She offered wise and memorable advice: "I know you want to stamp this out. But don't. Don't try to go around, go *through* it. I promise you it will not last forever, but give him the time he needs to work through it." Which, of course, was what our speech pathologist was already doing.

Though I didn't know the word for it at the time, Bryce is a *gestalt* learner. "Gestalt" is a German word that means "whole" or "complete." Gestalt learners take experiences as one piece, without being able to see the individual components. In the case of language development, children with ASD who tend to learn language in gestalt manner will absorb language in chunks, rather than as individual words. Neuro-typical young children also exhibit echolalia at some point in their development but outgrow it with the usual expansion of generative language skills. (Adults use it, too, on some level. Tell me you've never dared someone to "go ahead—make my day.") But many children with autism, such as gestalt learners and those with more limited spontaneous language ability, may linger in echolalia much longer. As opposed to gestalt, we call word-by-word learning "analytic." It may seem as though analytic language learners are more typical in the population than gestalt learners. In fact many children with ASD, particularly Asperger's, are analytic learners who can easily associate meaning with individual words. Both analytic and gestalt are legitimate ("normal") learning styles.

Marge Blanc, founder of the Communication Development Center in Madison, Wisconsin, describes the four stages of gestalt language acquisition:

The Stages of Gestalt Language Acquisition

Stage 1 - Communicative use of language gestalts (learned and spoken in their entirety)

"Let's get out of here!"

"Want some more?"

Stage 2 - Mitigation into chunks (a) and recombining (b)

(a)"Let's get + out of here!"

"Want + some more?"

(b)"Let's get some more!"

"Want out of here?"

Stage 3 - Isolation of single words and morphemes, and beginning generation of original two-word phrases

"Get . . . more!"

"Want . . . out?"

Stage 4 - Generation of more complex sentences

"I got more."

"I wanna go out?"

Source: "Finding the Words." *Autism Asperger's Digest*, May-June 2005.

A knowledgeable speech therapist is your child's guide through the process of learning to break apart "gestalts" and reconstruct the smaller pieces into spontaneous speech. As you embark upon this process, remember that each child will have a unique response pattern to language therapy. Not only is there no correct or typical timetable for moving through the four stages, but be aware that sometimes progress may look like regression. If your child has been spouting the vivid, eloquent language of movie and video scripts, his learning to generate simple, original sentences of his own (Stage 3) may temporarily sound rather toddler-esque. It's not. It's healthy language development.

In the meantime, it may ease some of your anxieties about your child's echolalia if you take time to notice how he uses it. Chances are, he isn't just "playing tapes" in his head, but his echolalia may be quite functional in a number of ways. Listen and note. See if he might use it to:

- Reciprocate conversation, provide a response where he knows an exchange is expected.

- Ask for or request something, either an object or someone's attention.

- Offer information or opinion.

- Protest or deny the actions or requests of others.

- Give instructions or directives.

- Put a name or a label to an item, activity or place.

These are functional, interactive uses of echolalia.

When Bryce was ten, I was stunned to learn that, upon testing, his vocabulary was considered severely subpar for a fourth-grader. Coming from almost a standing start with language at age four, I had grown very proud of his accomplishments with the spoken word, which included being completely at ease speaking in front of groups. I asked to see the test material. Among other things, he had failed to correctly identify words like *cactus, violin* and *bachelor*. At first, this brought my hackles up. Those three words represented things that he seldom, if ever, encountered in his daily life, or in his reading or movie viewing. And he had gotten the context correct: he had identified the picture of the cactus as a "desert plant" and the violin as a "music player." He didn't know the word "bachelor" but I knew he understood that a man who has no wife is not married, and vice versa. But even as I was annoyed at the imprecise nature of the testing (something about which I am frequently annoyed to distraction, but that's another book), it did make me begin to realize how extensively, in listening to and responding to him, I was automatically decoding the irregular language in both his spontaneous speech and in his echolalic utterances. I didn't want to spend all my conversational time with him correcting grammar and syntax, so I was simply doing the translation in my head and continuing to exchange thoughts with him uninterrupted.

In one sense, it was the right thing to do: I was validating his means of functional communication and with it, his self-image. But I took the test results as a good wake-up call that I needed to do just a bit more everyday "feeding in" of language as well as checking for comprehension in both the spoken and written word. For instance, while Bryce was still learning to read, we came across this passage in a story: "He ripped the handbag from her grasp." Bryce looked blank, so we stopped and I went over the words rip, grasp and handbag. "Oh," he said, with exasperation. "He stole her purse. Why doesn't it just say that? *He stole her purse?*"

This small incident led to a longer discussion of how words, like colors, come in many "shades" and how varying our words can make a story "colorful." We had a good time coming up with a long and comical list of all the ways to say *big*: large, huge, gigantic, immense, enormous, whopping, humongous, colossal, and on and on. It was a light bulb moment for both him and me. He simply hadn't thought of words that way, and I hadn't thought of offering them so. There's a jazzy name for this, *multiple descriptors*, and it took a bit of practice for me to get into the habit of using them. But in time I did learn to ditch the lazy shortcut, "Get your coat," and instead say "It's raining, so wear your red jacket with the hood today."

***

As a teen, Bryce has gotten very good at putting the "fun" in "functional." I knew he had reached the pinnacle of gestalt language acquisition when he asked me to listen to him practice asking a girl for a "someday" date. He had spent some time thinking of activities that girls might enjoy. Here is how it went: "Sometime if you would like to hang out with me, go to a movie or a picnic or the park, I would indeed be honored." Of course, the girls to whom he says this just love it. And they probably will never know that "I would indeed be honored" is a line straight out of the movie *Grumpier Old Men*.

Chapter Six

Because language is so difficult for me, **I am very visually oriented.**

One of my favorite spunky girls is *My Fair Lady's* Eliza Doolittle, a character created as a walking, breathing language experiment. She makes herself impossible to ignore in a number of ways, but never more so than in the song *Show Me*, when she admonishes her lover to knock it off with the "Words, words, words—I'm so sick of words!" followed by, "Don't waste my time—show me!"

Her sentiments would be cheered by more than a few children with autism.

Visual cuing is hardly a novelty, even in the neuro-typical world. If you carry a day-planner or keep a calendar on your desk or wall, you are already using a *visual schedule.* Sign language—I recently saw it called "handspeak"—is a highly developed form of visual communication that includes facial expression and body language in a manner similar to how vocal volume and inflection enhance the meaning of spoken language. *Semaphore* uses flag signals rather than words and letters to communicate visually across distances. Go to a baseball game and watch the third base coach rub his forearm, grab his belt and slap his chest. He's not auditioning for a Jane Goodall film. He's telling his base runner, without words, not to go unless the ball is a hopper to shallow right field. The common thread is that all these modes of interface use something other than spoken words to achieve functional communication.

Your child or student may have a profound need for visual cuing, and it likely stems from the fact that many individuals with autism think in images, not words. Their primary "language" is pictorial, not verbal. A child may have minimal verbal expressive language but are we really arrogant enough, or naive enough, to think that this means he has no thoughts, preferences, opinions, ideas or beliefs? *Does* that tree falling in the woods really make no sound because no one is around to hear it? Nonsense. Your child or student may be translating his life experiences into "video" in his head. It is a language no less legitimate than the one you use to speak, and it is the one you must accommodate if you want to be able to reach and teach him in a meaningful way that leads to meaningful results.

Temple Grandin elevated the world's awareness of the visual orientation of autism in her 1996 book *Thinking in Pictures*, which begins with this: "I think in pictures. Words are like a second language to me. I translate both spoken and written words into full-color movies, complete with sound, which run like a VCR tape in my head. When somebody speaks to me, his words are instantly translated into pictures. Language-based thinkers often find this phenomenon difficult to understand."

What should not be difficult to understand is that the ability to communicate, to receive and to express and to feel "heard," is fundamental to the overall healthy functioning of your child, of any person. Without an effective means of communicating, expect behavior consequences to follow. This is true even in the so-called real world, where we have a word for what happens when two parties fail, in the extreme, to communicate. It's called *war*. A visually oriented child (square peg) continually being squeezed into a verbally oriented world (round hole) is bound to feel unheard, embattled, overwhelmed and outnumbered. What should she do, but retreat?

Of course, not all children with ASD think in pictures. But the lovely thing about many visual tools is that they are beneficial for all kids. Bryce had an elementary school teacher who, through an earlier ASD student, was already familiar with visual schedules and excited about using them again. A large one posted by the door served the whole class; all the kids loved it and loved romping on the teacher if any little thing didn't get changed properly from day to day. It's also worth noting that most of the kids in this class finished the year without knowing exactly why my son's paraeducator was in the classroom. She did such a seamless job of supporting him while also assisting the rest of the class that many of the children ending up asking, "Why are you here?" ("To help you!") or "Why do we get two teachers?" ("Because you are very lucky and so am I! We get to spend this school year together, with Mrs. M, in her wonderful classroom!") Such skillful inclusion goes light years toward lowering the perception of "disability" for your child or student. The teacher's assessment of Bryce's visual schedule, paraeducator and other accommodations was, "It was critical for him but it was also good for the rest of the class."

Creating a visual schedule or other visual strategy to help your child navigate his school day or home routine may be one of the first tools suggested to you by your school team or by your own research. Why? It:

- Provides the structure and predictability so important to children with autism. Knowing what is going to happen frees her to focus on the task or activity at hand without the anxiety of worrying about what comes next and when.

- Provides a touchstone—a consistent source of information that makes it possible for her to trust that events will unfold logically and she can feel safe in that routine.

- Reinforces the "first/then" strategy for dealing with less enjoyable tasks. When he can see that finishing his math leads to computer time, he can feel motivated rather than lapsing into avoidance or procrastination.

- Increases his ability to perform tasks autonomously and to transition between activities independently.

- Can help ease the rigidity of thinking and inflexibility that frequently characterize autism. As the child's confidence in his independence grows, "curveballs" can be inserted into the schedule in the form of varied activities, or even a question mark, indicating a surprise activity.

- Can incorporate social skill-building. The schedule might include a five-minute "play [or read] with a classmate" time or "say or wave goodbye to three people."

All of this aids immeasurably in your child's or student's ability to understand and meet the expectations of those around him.

All visual schedules are not created equal any more than all calendars are. The common element is their sequential nature. But beyond that, the size, style of representation, portability and length are all negotiable.

When Bryce started out with a visual schedule, he was in preschool and the prevailing medium was Boardmasters, a system of simple line-drawing stick-figures depicting various activities. We had a lot of little laminated squares with Velcro® on the back that we could arrange in a strip to make up the day's routine: get up, eat breakfast, get dressed, brush teeth, get on bus. He would do each task, then remove the picture, drop it in an attached envelope and move on to the next thing. It worked after a fashion but he never seemed very engaged in it. It was a year or so later when I realized that Bryce did not relate to artwork, especially fanciful or unrealistic artwork. He liked concrete depictions – photographs. Stick figures had little meaning for him. He became much more engaged when I presented stories, instructions, etc., with photographs.

So, the first step in setting up a successful visual communication strategy is to know your child or student's "level of representation." That's fancy talk for determining what is visually meaningful to him. For Bryce, it was photographs. For another child, it might be stick figures, pencil drawings or full-color art. As the child gets older, it might be words in combination with pictures, and finally, words alone (then it gets called a "To-Do List").

Consider the following as well: how does your child best track information? Do not assume it is left to right. It may be top to bottom. An occupational therapist can help you determine this. How many increments should be on a schedule or a page at any one time? Don't overwhelm—you can always start with three and work up from there.

Visual strategies are not something to be phased out as your child becomes progressively more independent. Over time, I keep coming up against gentle reminders that a visual schedule is much more than a strip of stick-figure sketches that we used to help Bryce learn to get ready for pre-school. The level of representation and sophistication may escalate with the years, but not the need, and not the stability it provides and the stress it relieves. Again, it's what keeps the calendar printers and palm-pilot designers in business.

At the beginning of middle school, in a new building full of new teachers and a sea of new faces, Bryce faced a formidable challenge. Outdoor School is a popular long-standing program in our county wherein all sixth graders go to local camps for a week to learn about native ecosystems; a terrific program, but one that raised many questions on both my part and Bryce's. He had never spent five nights away from home without family. He would be under the supervision of two teachers who had known him less than six weeks (it was October), and the rest of the camp staff, who didn't know him at all. He would have to tolerate unfamiliar routine, unpredictable weather, sleeping and eating with children he had never met before—and perhaps worst of all—"camp food."

Although both school and camp staff assured me they would make any accommodation necessary, Bryce wasn't sure he wanted to go, changing his mind from hour to hour as he worried about it all. We drove up to the camp for visitation, through which he remained stoically silent. He surveyed the dining room, which would be, he was sure, a source of much suffering. But wait—he shows a spark of interest! On the wall by the door, literally larger than life, is the daily schedule: 6:45 wake up, 7:15 flag, 7:30 breakfast, 10:30 wildlife studies, 11:15 lunch, 12:00 quiet time, 5:00 dinner, 5:45 songs, 6:30 campfire and class meeting, etc. The whole day was mapped out in manageable increments.

"Would somebody get me a copy of this?" he asked.

I'm certain of it, I told him. And they did—and punched a hole in it and hung it around his neck on a lanyard, too. Before he left he also asked me for the meal-by-meal schedule I had gotten from the head cook, so that he would know exactly when he was eating camp food and when he would be asking for one of the special meals I sent up with him.

Bryce's teacher reported that he had easily settled in—armed with his two, frequently consulted visual schedules—within twenty-four hours. This had been an important accommodation. They provided predictability and a concrete routine that made the exotic, potentially intimidating setting not only manageable but enjoyable. He organized and directed his cabin's skit, a spoof on the morning inspection routine. At the final campfire, he made his teacher cry as he spoke movingly about feeling unsure when he arrived but "making new friends" throughout the week. He wore the same pair of socks the entire week and ignored the other five pairs in his bag. He had a *typical* Outdoor School experience and he spent the rest of the year telling anyone who asked that it was the very best part of sixth grade.

The really important thing to remember is that in order for teaching to be effective, you must be heard, and many children with autism simply "hear" better with a picture. Also recognize that what happens between the words and the picture is translation. You may need to slow down your usual pace of communication to allow that processing to happen. Give her extra time to respond, don't repeat the same instructions over and over if they clearly are not getting through. "Please don't 'expline!'" Eliza Doolittle scolds. "Show me!"

Any communication that doesn't make sense to the recipient simply won't get through. For so many children with ASD, visuals make sense where words don't. Picture it (get it?) this way: pictures are the powerful medium that takes your child's world and organizes it, explains it, tames its stress, gives him understandable guidance and boundaries. See it his way—teach him in a way that makes sense to *him*. Life then becomes less of a battle; he need be less of a warrior. He comes, he sees—he conquers.

Chapter Seven

Focus and build on what I can do rather than what I can't do.

When the "Ten Things" article was first published, my brother commented, "Number seven is true for all kids." And, of course, he is right. I would even extend it to all people, not just kids.

Yet many families and educators unwittingly and unhappily tumble into the Swamp of Unmet Expectations. This is where a child's potential goes to die if we as adults are not successful in detaching our personal aspirations from those appropriate for our child.

Our adapted PE teacher sees it all the time: "Parents get into a grieving process: their child isn't going to be a certain way that they expected her to be, and it's a huge handicap for the child. I see many cases where the parent may be very much into physical fitness and sports. Their too-high expectations in that area can turn the child completely off to the very things the parent wants him to be. I see these children every week; they don't care a hoot for PE." They may have skills very similar to developmentally "regular" kids, she says, but the processing of those skills is different, and it all means nothing without a belief system behind it. "I can tell them for years, I know you can do this! But if they don't have that full parental support, there is only so much I can do in only thirty minutes a week."

I get to say again here that I am no fan of politically correct doublespeak. So without invoking the pretentious phrase "differently abled," let's nevertheless agree that there is something to consider in the comparison between what constitutes a *disability* and what constitutes a *different ability*. We are all differently abled. As George Carlin puts it, "Barry Bonds can't play the cello and Yo Yo Ma can't hit the curveball." My husband can't write books and I can't engineer industrial air flow systems. It never comes up for discussion; we're just happy knowing that our different skills and abilities mean we each have a constructive place in the world.

My mail is full of sad stories that echo the can't-do lament of parents, but nevertheless have potential for happy endings. "Four generations of Andersons have played the violin, and I can't even get him to look at one!" No kidding. Is there a musical instrument more sensory-hellish than a violin? Imagine the screechy sound every new learner produces, the strings that bite into tender fingers and the sensation of having a weirdly shaped vibrating box parked under your sweaty chin while you hold both arms up at unnatural angles! It took someone outside this family to notice that the child, while not musical, was a complete natural on the golf course, with an amazing, easy and accurate swing. I hope this family took the opportunity to not only learn something new from their child but to validate his capability as well.

Another family, passionate skiers, gloomily accepted that their child's vestibular issues made skiing and snowboarding abhorrent to him. But while at the beach one summer, Mom noticed her son could spend hours moving piles of sand around, examining them from every angle, making structural adjustments. She wasn't quite sure what he was seeing but that winter she bought him a set of snow block molds (basically, just plastic boxes) and away he went building igloos, forts and castles. Her discovery of what he could do rather than what he couldn't do meant that the family could still spend a day together on the mountain, with each family member rotating "Andy time" with the snow forts while the others skied. Eventually, Andy acclimated to the snow enough to try gentle innertubing and a bit of snowshoeing. Someday I may see him up there on Nordic skis.

So much of being able to focus and build on the can-do rather than can't-do of your child has to do with perspective —yours. Earlier in the book we talked about reframing some of your child's challenging behaviors as positives. It bears repeating. Is the child standoffish—or able to work well independently? Is he reckless—or adventuresome and willing to try new experiences? Is he obsessively neat—or does he have outstanding organizational skills? Do you hear nonstop pestering with questions—or do you see curiosity, tenacity and persistence?

Can you do this? *Will* you do this?

In the beginning, my father would marvel to me about what a happy baby Bryce was. "I have never, ever known a happier baby," he would say. "And I've been around a lot of babies." It was true; Bryce was so sweet and placid. He went everywhere with me.

At age two, he starts a preschool program two mornings a week, and the wheels start to come off almost immediately. September isn't even over before the teacher reports that Bryce plays only in a corner by himself, his language skills are underdeveloped, he doesn't participate in "table" activities and he perpetrates minor aggression, hitting or pushing another child. It's extremely hard to believe because it is so out of character. By spring conference time, things seem precarious. "Bryce usually plays by himself," states the written report (again). "Clean-up after activities is a difficult task for Bryce. He's quiet and will observe other children. He has a hard time following directions. Bryce doesn't like art projects or table activities. He says words but we have a hard time understanding him. He imitates the other children. Bryce has a short attention span. He doesn't interact during circle time."

Wow, I thought. That's a damn lot of can'ts. He's *two*.

The recitation of can't/doesn't carried into the next year. At November parent conferences, I politely interrupted the teacher to ask if we could refocus on some things that Bryce can do and is doing. With this prompt, I heard how he was content to entertain himself for long periods, loved physical play whether indoors or out, sought out sand table play and had some gift for imitation. All factors combined to suggest that his difficulties with language were interfering substantially with his ability to become a part of the classroom community. I thought, here is something I *can do*, and we entered the world of private speech therapy. Soon, he was putting together intelligible three-word phrases at school.

Still, even my asking for *cans* and enlisting professional help didn't change the big picture. The winter report was by now wearyingly familiar: wants to interact with other children but doesn't know how, sits for long periods playing by himself, has a hard time listening in a group situation. I felt it was time to stop the spinning. I asked for a meeting with the teachers and the school principal. After listening yet again to the same *can'ts*, a touchy exchange unfolded in which I asked the teacher flat out if maybe she just didn't like Bryce. She reacted as if she'd been shot. I instantly felt crummy-and-a-half, wondering if I had poisoned all the productivity out of the meeting. No, said the principal, that is a legitimate question; you had to ask. The answer was this: they all *loved* Bryce—but his needs were simply beyond their ability to handle within the resources of the school. The meeting ended with the principal's decision to refer him to public Early Intervention services.

What is that? I ask, having never heard the term "early intervention." What is happening?

They are people who will help, she said.

The Early Intervention teachers and therapists were amazing can-do people right from the start. They continually told me how "cool" Bryce was, how far they thought he could go, why they thought so and how we chart the journey to get there. But the earliest books I read on the subject were another story. I read in earnest, and quite a lot of what I read was dismal. He won't form relationships, won't get married, won't be able to hold a job, won't understand the nuances of the law or the banking system or the bus system—won't, won't, won't. There it was on the page in black and white, yet more nay-saying, written by people who supposedly knew a lot more than I did. I am not, I told myself, in denial. But already, deep in the space between the gray matter and the heart, a tiny voice strained to be heard. *Don't believe it. It isn't true unless you let it be.* I was just starting out but I was already done listening to "can't."

One of the most important things you can do as a parent is to heed the strong inner voice that tells you what is right for your child. No one else loves her like you do and no one else is as invested in her future. The most popular treatments and thinking of the day may be right for many children but may not be for yours. One particular approach to autism was extremely prevalent in the early 1990s when Bryce was first identified. I read about it, *loathed* it, knew with 200% certainty that it was wrong for Bryce and during a very memorable school meeting, told those wonderful early intervention people: "Do this to my kid and I will kill you." Happily for me, they had already decided the same thing (the teacher later told me she wanted to stand up and applaud). Most of them are still in my life, cherished friends, and boy, do they remember that conversation. It gets revisited on a regular basis.

Taking the can-do attitude rather than the can't-do approach to autism is one of the biggest general shifts I've seen in the ten years since Bryce was identified. My can-do attitude about him is strong now, but it is a result of my early confrontations with can't-do: the can't-do messages I received about him did scare me, *of course* they scared me. But they are also challenged me, made me mad, made me say, "Oh yeah? Well, we'll just see about that."

If you haven't been in the habit of consciously—and conscientiously—focusing on what your child *can* do, how do you start? First, acknowledge that this is a shift in mindset, and it will take time and practice. Next, look for an indication of your child's learning style; there are many. Typically developing children may learn in a variety of ways, but for children with autism, one learning style may be favored almost to exclusion of all others. *Sequential learners* benefit from step-by-step instructions, are frequently good at rote memorization, may be "neat freaks" (they like visual organization). *Gestalt* or global learners, assimilate information in chunks, looking at the big picture first, then chunking it down into details. *Naturalist learners* learn best in natural settings among naturally-occurring elements. They like to interact with natural surroundings and may demonstrate an unusual ability to categorize, organize or preserve information. Call it advanced sorting skills. *Kinesthetic learners* "learn by doing," seeking to experience the world through large and small movement of their bodies. They are climbers, runners, dancers, actors; they enjoy crafts and tools. The *spatial learner* is your little construction worker or chess player. He likes to plan and/or build and draw things he sees in his head and seems to have an inborn understanding of concepts of physics and geometry, but may be poor at spelling and memorizing verbal passages. Many children with autism who are hypersensitive to noise and have delayed verbal skills may be *musical learners.* They perceive patterns in sound (rhythms, rhymes, raps), hold melodies in their heads and compose their own tunes as mnemonic devices.

These are just a few types of learning styles that might characterize your child with autism. Once you have this understanding of how she processes information, the flood gates to learning are open. You'll be much better able to guide her through activities inside and outside of school that she "can do" and experience the confidence-building success to eventually confront some of the "can't-do's." You'll be more flexible and enthusiastic in your approach, and you'll see it in the increased enthusiasm she will have for learning because now, finally, it makes some sense to her!

In doing so, you *must* throw out conventional or typical growth charts and timelines that you may see in books or doctors' offices. Much of it is irrelevant to your child. At the outset of my journey, I was told that one of the hallmarks of autism was "uneven development." One of Bryce's early friends was a four-year-old oceanography wiz who had forgotten more about coral reef habitats and bioluminescence than I will ever know. But his mother told me she would trade it all for a few moments of eye contact and a smile like Bryce's. I hope that by now she's got both.

Bryce does have a brilliant smile, but the conventional timelines have been meaningless for him in most ways. He didn't talk reliably until age four, and didn't read reliably until the fourth grade. He loved swimming pools, but he was a devout barnacle, clinging to the sides, steadfastly refusing swim lessons until age eight when all of a sudden, with the right teacher and the right pool, he "got it" and churned through all six levels of the swim program in a matter of a few months. It's worth noting that his "0-60 in six seconds" achievement in learning to swim is not typical, either. His instructors told us that most kids would invariably get stuck at a certain level, sometimes for months, before moving on. Like his language development, Bryce learned to swim in a gestalt manner—big but delayed chunks rather than the more typical progression of little steps.

And now a word about our responsibilities and vulnerabilities as parents, family members and teachers in all of this: One of the most distressing Internet posts I ever read was on a site whose members had posted my "Ten Things" and were having a colorful discussion about it. One mom, who admitted she was "tired and snarky," wrapped up a long I-love-you-*but* message to her child with this: "Oh, and God, if you're listening, I take back what I stupidly vowed when she was small and adorable and didn't hit me, about not wanting her any other way than what she was—I'll take that trade-in now, for the kid she was supposed to be."

I wanted to both weep and rage when I read this because I am beyond certain that her child doesn't sit around asking God if she can trade in her mother for the parent she was "supposed" to be. I weep for all the everyday magic she will miss in her child, the opportunities and accomplishments drowned in the stew of bitterness. I rage at the no-win situation in which she's placed her child, the unfairness of blaming autism for even the regular-kid things she does: "Don't feed almonds and Barbie parts to the dog. I don't appreciate the extra mess."

But even though this mother's soul-crushing fatigue was palpable and even though most of her post was snarly in tone, I could still pick out the building blocks of hope that had the power to turn the whole thing around. She worried for the future of her child as an adult and she wanted to lessen the impact of her child's autism on the siblings ("so that when we are gone . . . they won't immediately associate you with stealing their childhoods, and relegate you to the worst institution the state has available"). She was engaging her child in therapies such as OT and speech (albeit referred to as "tortures"); she was weighing the pros and cons of medications. So even though her words were harsh and made me cringe, I can hope that she finds her way to building on what both she and her child *can* do.

If you are treading quicksand in the swamp of what-might-have-been, you can be pretty sure that's the message your child is getting. You're a rare person if being constantly reminded of your shortcomings spurs you to improve. For the rest of us, it's not a self-esteem-building experience. Time to grab for that overhead vine and realize that there is only a pencil stroke's difference between "bitter" and "better."

As parents (and family members and teachers), we do need to reflect this advice about can-do and can't-do back on ourselves, too. When a diagnosis or identification of autism first comes in, many parents feel overwhelming urgency. They rush to read everything about autism they can get their hands on, join online discussion groups and network like mad with other parents. And sometimes the ensuing crush of information overwhelms. There is so much to absorb; some of it is encouraging and uplifting and some of it is depressing and spirit-sapping. There are professionals to consult, school and therapy programs that need to be put into action, medications and special diets to consider and worries about how to pay for all of it. If you allow yourself to be overtaken by the avalanche of new information descending upon you, you risk overdosing on the very tools that are going to get you through the long haul ahead. Paralysis sets in. It's real; it happens.

Here is one thing you "can do." Adjust yourself to this new challenge at a measured, reasonable pace by knowing this:

You have some time. You have lots of time.

You have today.

You have tomorrow.

You have next week.

You have next month and next year, and many years after that.

Every passing year brings new information and understanding, for you and for the fields of medicine and education.

Stay the course: therapies, strategies, treatments and all. Results will come.

Chapter Eight

Please help me with social interactions.

We can be blunt with each other here. Kids with ASD frequently stand out as social oddballs. The heartbreak it causes, to child and maybe even more so to parent, is the very reason many parents feel the intense need to "fix" that aspect of their child. If social competence was a physiological function, we could throw medication, nutrition, exercise or physical therapy at it and make it happen. If our kids were curious, outgoing, motivated learners, we could teach it curriculum-style.

But our kids aren't like that, and social awareness isn't a set of concrete, itemized skills. "Manners" (please and thank you, use Kleenex® not sleeve, wait your turn) can be taught but learning to be at ease among others in the bustle and nuances of daily life isn't something that comes from a book. It is more a state of confident being that grows with careful nurturing of several important character traits:

- Flexibility—being able to see and experience the world from standpoints other than your own, being able to "roll" with unforeseen deviations from routine and expectation, being able to recognize that mistakes are part of learning and that disappointments are matters of degree.

- Motivation—the impetus that we get from not only understanding that something exists, but why its existence is important and how it matters to us.

- Self-esteem—having enough faith in your own abilities to be able to risk trying new things, to experience failure as part of learning and growing rather than as an end result. Having enough respect and affection for yourself to be able to deflect the cruel and thoughtless remarks and actions of others as saying more about them than you.

- Awareness of nonverbal communication—These are the junctures at which the complex subtleties of social interaction can go awry. There are three broad categories:

  - Vocalic communication: He doesn't "get" the myriad nuances of spoken language. He doesn't understand sarcasm, puns, idioms, metaphors, hints, slang, double entendres, hyperbole, or abstraction. He may speak in a monotone (suggesting boredom to the listener), or he may speak too loudly, too softly, too quickly or too slowly.

  - Kinesthetic communication: He doesn't understand body language, facial expressions, or emotional responses (crying, recoiling). He may use gestures or postures inappropriately and may refuse eye contact.

  - Proxemic communication: He doesn't understand physical space communication, the subtle territorial cues and norms of personal boundaries. He may be an unwitting "space invader." The rules of proxemics not only vary from culture to culture, but from person to person depending upon relationship: Intimate? Casual but personal? Social only? Public space? For most ASD kids, deciphering proxemics requires an impossible level of inference.

There's no short cut, magic bullet or eureka cure to your child's becoming comfortable with social interaction. It's a mosaic of thousands upon thousands of petite opportunities and encounters that coalesce into a core of self-confidence. It requires you, as his parent, his teacher, his guide, to be socially aware for him 110% of the time and clue him into the social nuances that are so difficult for him to perceive.

Social navigation is necessary at every turn in our lives: at home, at work, at school, in our travels about the community, in our shopping, recreation and worship. As you shepherd your child through this challenging landscape, I implore you: do it without the mindset that you must "fix" him. Sending the child a constant message that he needs to be "fixed" will surely build the wall that prevents the very progress we want for him. Self-esteem, that essential component of social functioning, will not flourish in an environment that sends the message: *You're not good enough just the way you are.* Certainly there may be behaviors that aren't conducive to his social development, but always, always separate the behavior from the whole child.

With Bryce, I knew unequivocally, coming off the blocks, that we were in a long, long race and that the finish line, if in fact there was one, was light years distant. On a good day, it meant the routine unfolded pleasantly and productively and that progress toward our goals was evident. On a bad day it meant that life had to be lived not one day at a time, but one moment at a time.

It was on one of those days when the road stretched too far ahead that I began to wonder, how much is enough? When the need is as all-encompassing and as never-ending as is the constellation of social skills, how would I know where the teaching and nurturing of those skills would cross the line into the "repair" mode? Where lay the boundary between providing my son the galaxy of services and opportunities he needed and—well, bombardment? He was barely five years old and was putting in rigorous 6-1/2 hour days at school in a developmental kindergarten with afternoon inclusion, speech therapy three days a week, adaptive PE and one-on-one occupational therapy. Yes, we could make the rounds of after-school supplemental therapies, tutorings and social activities. But I began to have serious, serious misgivings about what sort of message it was sending.

Something is "wrong" with me.

On the day I first became a mother, our pediatrician told me: "Trust your instincts. You know more than you think you know." Now I chose to follow that advice; I pulled Bryce out of everything but school. I did it because I came to believe that the manner in which he was taught, the pace at which he was taught and the context in which he was taught were as equal parts of the skill-building equation as the skill itself. Force-feeding without creating relevance would bring forth a gag response. The environment in which he would best be able to learn was not one of incessant pressure and demand. It was more important for me to create that foundation where self-esteem could flourish and he could come to genuinely like himself and be comfortable inside his own skin. With those underpinnings, I believed the social skills would come. But they would come on his unique timetable, not one that I or others had lifted from books or charts or comparisons to other children. I wasn't at all sure I was doing the right thing, but with Bryce there did seem to be a direct relationship between pacing and his self-esteem. His "down" time was actually his "recharging" time; it enabled him to exercise some choice over a portion of his life and consequently, to be willing to give 100% at school. "*Bravo*," said his paraeducator. "You wouldn't believe how many exhausted kids I see. Like all kids, they need time to just be kids."

Bryce, who at thirteen has succeeded at social interaction in settings ranging from team sports to school dances, is a grand example of what a child with autism can achieve when healthy self-esteem leads the way. We are ten years into this expedition. How many, many miles along the spectrum we have traveled to get here, sometimes trudging, sometimes tripping the light fantastic. In hindsight I can see that my relentless reinforcing of his self-esteem was the single biggest factor in his willingness to be nudged out of his comfort zone. It also expanded his comfort zone enormously. He has the jaw-dropping—for *any* kid—ability to deflect teasing and cruelty with the perspective that the insulter "needs to work on his manners" or "has some growing up to do."

Teaching social awareness is infinitely easier if you separate and clarify your goals, address only one goal at a time, start small and build upon incremental successes. Remove obstacles (usually sensory, language or self-esteem issues) and throw out preconceived, stereotypical measures of what constitutes progress—the definition of which is sure to be a moving target.

Separating goals and keeping them manageable is of the essence, because where messages overlap, you can't look to your child to be able to sort the primary goal from the secondary one. If you want your child to be a pleasant, involved member of the family at dinner, recognize that several goals are involved in this situation. To isolate the social component, you may need to provide appropriate seating and utensils for him, eliminate foods (his and others') that offend him sensorily, or make concerted efforts to include him in the conversation. Ensure that dinner is not for him an exercise in unpleasant smells and enforced two-bite tastings, lectures about manners and the incomprehensible jabbering of the group. If the goal is socialization, separate it from food goals or fine motor processing goals. I've had to walk that walk. At various times in my kids' lives, they ate breakfast in their rooms. The commotion of the morning routine was too much for them, and the goal at that time of day was nutrition, not socialization. It was a temporary accommodation that lasted a few months, not forever. It was one of many accommodations we made along the way. And let me tell you where all of this patient separation of goals got us. My birthday, the year Bryce was twelve, found us celebrating as a family in one of the most elegant white-tablecloth restaurants in town. The boys loved it, and I will experience very few moments more magical than watching Bryce stride confidently up to the piano bar, $5 tip in hand, and asking the piano man, "Could you please play 'Stardust' for my mom? It's her birthday." All the many years of patient acclimation just melted away.

There's no pill or potion for instilling social capability. It builds, phoenix-like, upon itself particle by particle, day by day. "To the top of the mountain, one step at a time," advises the old proverb. We're not Moses, so there won't be tablets at the summit—if in fact there is a summit—but if there were they might look something like this:

1. Eradicate the thought of "fix."

2. Build your child's self-esteem as a foundation for social risk-taking and a shield against the unkindness of others.

3. Create circumstances in which she can succeed in social settings; not intermittently, not just occasionally, but constantly.

4. Be specific in defining your social skill goals, and beware of goals that overlap or conflict.

5. Keep your teaching increments small; build as you go.

6. Maintain an open-ended definition of what constitutes progress. Two steps forward/one step back is still growth to be celebrated.

7. Provide a reasonable "out" for risk-taking situations. You want him to try the church choir or after-school Lego club or volunteering at the pet shelter, but if after several sessions he absolutely hates it, let him know it's okay to stop, and move on to something else. Save "sticking it out" for matters of greater consequence.

8. Provide lots of opportunities to practice social skills.

9. Instill flexibility in thinking. Not every mistake or disappointment is a big deal; emotions exist in degrees.

10. One word, three times over: patience, patience, patience. Just as they do for you, some days will go better for your child than others will.

Understand and keep in mind that fitting into our social world requires a tremendous amount of effort on your child's part—always. He's trying the best he can with the abilities and social understanding he has. Despite the social nuances he doesn't get, what he does know is when you believe in him and when that belief falters.

"To the top of the mountain, one step at a time." When my son Connor was young, one of his favorite stories was that of Sir Edmund Hillary and his Sherpa guide Tenzing Norgay, the first people ever to reach the summit of Mt. Everest. We talked a lot about the controversy over the years regarding which one of them had actually put their foot on the top first. Although there is much speculation that it was actually Tenzing and not the more famous Sir Edmund Hillary, Tenzing's son Jamling told Forbes magazine in an interview in 2001: "I did ask him—and he said, 'You know, it's not important, Jamling. We climbed as a team.'" Like Tenzing, you've been climbing this mountain for many years. Like Hillary, your child is making his first ascent. Be his Sherpa, knowing and helping him see that the view along the way can be spectacular.

Chapter Nine

Try to identify what triggers my meltdowns.

Here is something you may not believe but will by the end of this chapter: there are many, many reasons why a child with autism melts down, blows up, loses it, goes crackerdog. Being bratty, petulant, obstinate or spoiled is so far down the list of possibilities that I can't even see it without my binoculars.

We've already looked at the unvarnished bottom line, but here it is again: all behavior springs from a reason, and all behavior is communication. A meltdown is a clear message from a child who is at that moment not able to tell you in any other way: something is happening in his environment that has caused his delicate neurology to go haywire. Even the child whose verbal skills are adequate in an ordinary setting can "lose his voice" in the midst of stressful moments. For the limited-verbal or nonverbal child, there may truly be no other choice, particularly if there is no alternate functional communication system available to him. But regardless of the child's verbal skills level, it will be easier for you to keep your wits about you if you remember, always, that *it is not within his control. He does not make a conscious choice to throw a tantrum.* Thinking for even a moment that the child somehow wants the kind of negative attention he gets from a meltdown is illogical and counterproductive.

Square one for us has to be the belief that this child would interact appropriately if only he could, but has neither the social cognition, the sensory integrative abilities nor the language to achieve it. If this is not your current mind-set, it may take conscious practice to get there. But with practice, the assumption that there is a trigger and the curiosity and tenacity to look for it can become second nature. Many other ideas we've talked about in this book come together here: sensory overload, *can't vs. won't*, inade-quate expressive speech. As you look for triggers, never forget that whatever the underlying cause, it is highly likely that your child cannot articulate it.

When I say all behavior has a *reason*, I mean an explana-tion, an underlying cause. Seeking out reasons can be labo-rious and challenging. It is not the same as coming up with an excuse for the behavior. An *excuse* is merely an attempt at justification, and may or may not have any truth behind it. President Kennedy urged us to "never accept difficulties as an excuse." I would turn that around and say, "Never make up excuses for difficulty." Really look at this state-ment:

"He just doesn't want to. He could (behave/sit still/coop-erate) if he wanted to."

See how it lets the speaker off the hook, excuses him or her from the harder work of finding an underlying cause? How many, many times we've heard that supposedly inspir-ing cliché, "You can do anything if you want to badly enough." Right. That is why so many people can fly, or live to be 300 years old. Can a blind child "just" copy off the blackboard, if he wanted to badly enough? If that sounds familiar—good. Because we are back at chapter three, dis-tinguishing between *won't* and *can't*. Lack of motivation isn't always the reason for noncompliance. All the motiva-tion in the world may still require patient, sustained instruc-tion and/or assistive technology. We can't (and won't!) use "he just doesn't want to" as the rationalization for turning away from more arduous but more effective intervention.

Many will be the wearying moment when the root cause of your child's meltdown will not be immediately evident. There may never be a time in your life when it is more incumbent upon you to become a detective. And don't go turning that into a comic book word. If you get out your dusty old thesaurus from sophomore English, you find lots of synonyms for "detect": ascertain, become aware of, diagnose, discover, expose, ferret out. Choose one, any of them will work. The good news is that baffling behaviors always have a root cause so you will not be tilting at windmills, Don Quixote-style, and your quest is certainly not an Impossible Dream. But it does require that you be detailed, curious and thorough in your search for that cause. You must be biology detective, psychology detective and environmental detective. I'm surprised somebody hasn't made a television show like this yet; it would certainly be more useful than—well, never mind.

Meltdown triggers tend to cluster into several areas. If you can pinpoint the trigger, you can prevent the meltdown, which is vastly preferable to trying to interrupt or extinguish it once it's in progress (rarely possible). Think of the old Chinese adage: give a man a fish and he eats for a day; teach him how to fish and he eats for a lifetime. Your ability to identify your child's triggers is the first step in helping him identify them himself. Self-regulation can follow, and there he goes, three steps further down the Yellow Brick Road to successful independence.

Let's look at four trigger clusters:

1. Sensory overload

2. Physical/physiological triggers:

- Food allergies or sensitivities

- Sleep disorders

- Gastrointestinal problems

- Inadequate nutrition

- Biochemical imbalances

- Unarticulated illness or injury

3. Emotional triggers

- Frustration

- Disappointment

- Maltreatment

- Sense of unfairness

4. Poor examples from adults

1. Sensory overload

(As discussed throughout this book, always look for sensory issues first.)

It's my birthday and the celebration is at a relative's home, a familiar place to Bryce. Nevertheless, halfway through the evening he begins to career through the house, clearly agitated, and when I attempt to calm him, his arms lash wildly, raking cat-like scratches around my face. Time to go, too soon, but that's the way it is, so I begin to gather up coats and toys. Wait, says a usually very understanding relative. Are you going to let a three-year-old dictate the evening to the rest of the family? I know what he's saying—it's my birthday and I deserve a little special attention once in a while, too. But the answer to his question is both yes and no. Yes, the three-year-old's needs are going to detour the evening. It doesn't negate that we had a lovely time up to that point. But no, he is not "dictating." He is communicating. Because his verbal language isn't there yet, I have to look for meaning in his behavior. The aggression drains out of him as soon as we leave. He was not being petulant. He was in pain.

The moral of this story is, I automatically assumed something was hurting him. It never occurred to me that he would be trying to ruin my evening. That would have been illogical—he was in a familiar place with people he knew, loved and normally enjoyed. Clearly, something was amiss. Too much unfiltered noise? A different, quease-inducing smell? Overtired, too many people? I didn't know—it didn't matter. The most important thing was to end the discomfort before it became the last thing remembered/first thing associated with that venue.

2. Physical/physiological triggers

• Food Allergies and Sensitivities

These are sometimes used in the same breath, but they are not the same thing. An *allergy* is a disordered immune-system response. A *sensitivity* is a drug-like reaction to a substance, the degree of response to which varies from person to person (e.g., two red jelly beans may incite hyper or aggressive behavior in one child, whereas another may be able to tolerate a handful). There is plenty of evidence that both can cause difficult or belligerent behavior in children. The list of possible offending substances is endless but some of the common culprits are food dyes, preservatives and other additives, milk, nuts, strawberries, citrus, shellfish, eggs, wheat, corn and soy.

Detection: Keep a food diary of everything your child eats for a week, making note of times when behaviors exhibit. If you begin to see a pattern of difficult behavior after the lunchtime peanut butter sandwich, you might begin by eliminating wheat or nuts from your child's diet for two weeks. Eliminate only one substance at a time; phase it out slowly if it's a major favorite. Did behaviors diminish after elimination of the food? Test your results by reintroducing a small amount of the food, gradually increasing the "dose," seeing if the behavior returns.

• Sleep Disorders

Your child's sleep disorders can suck you under, too. Behavior problems are sure to follow the child who is chronically exhausted.

Detection: If you've already tried the usual tactics— setting an inviolable bedtime routine, elimination of naps, "spraying for monsters," avoiding overstimulation, etc.—consider our now-familiar nemesis, sensory problems. Could it be:

- Noisy clocks, furnaces or plumbing?

- Scratchy sheets, blankets or pajamas?

- Competing smells of laundry products and toiletries?

- Proprioceptive insecurity? She may feel "lost in space" in her bed. A mummy-style sleeping bag, guardrail, tent or canopy with privacy curtains or tent might help.

- Gastrointestinal Problems

  For reasons not yet well enough understood, children with autism seem to experience a higher than typical instance of misery-inducing gastrointestinal problems, and your child may be voicing her pain through extreme behavior. Acid reflux (heartburn) can cause esophageal pain, sleep disruption and abdominal discomfort. Constipation and its complications (impaction, encopresis), diarrhea and chronic flatulence have social as well as physiological implications. More serious illnesses such as Crohn's disease, ulcerative colitis and irritable bowel syndrome (IBS) require ongoing medical supervision. The nonverbal or minimally verbal child's inability to articulate her suffering or cooperate with typical testing are reasons why far too many children go undiagnosed.

- Inadequate Nutrition

  Remember the old computer term "GIGO"— garbage in, garbage out? A child may be eating a lot, but if it is of low nutritive value, his brain may be literally starving, acutely affecting his behavior. An easy way to improve nutrition is to become conscious of eating foods closer to their "original" condition. Processed white flour and white sugar products, processed meats and fruit-flavored drink products are largely nutrient-low while high in fat, salt, sugar and chemicals.

Detection: As with allergy identification, make dietary changes slo-o-o-owly. A kamikaze-style wipeout of your child's favorite foods is a guaranteed recipe for failure. If behavior is deteriorating early in the day, could skipping breakfast be the culprit?

- Biochemical Imbalances

  This can include anything and everything: too much/not enough stomach acid, bile irregularities, vitamin or mineral deficiencies, even yeast or bacterial imbalance. Symptoms can include anxiety, depression, aggression, weight fluctuations, sleep problems, phobias and skin problems.

- Unarticulated illness or injury

  Ear infections and broken bones are but two examples of excruciatingly painful conditions that may be impossible for a child with limited verbal ability to adequately communicate.

3. Emotional triggers

  - Frustration

Frustration comes when she's trying but not able to meet your (or her own) expectations and goals. Maybe she does not understand the expectation, or maybe it is too high, unachievable. Maybe it is achievable but she doesn't understand why it is necessary or relevant, or maybe she doesn't have the social, motor or language skills to accomplish it.

I'll never forget a story I heard years ago about a little whirling dervish of a girl with ADHD, nine years old. Her teacher proposed a deal, a reward for meeting a behavioral goal. If the girl could "be good" for three weeks, the teacher would buy her an ice cream cone. The girl reported to her therapist: "Is she kidding? I can't even 'be good' for three hours, let alone three weeks. And besides, *I don't even like ice cream.*"

The goal: unrealistic, out of reach.

Guidance offered to help in accomplishing the goal: none.

The reward: irrelevant, and nowhere near equal in value to the effort required.

Here's a scenario that is better times six: Teacher and student (1) meet one-on-one and (2) discuss and agree to (3) a specific, (4) short-range goal (5) that is reasonable and (6) has a meaningful motivator as a reward. For instance, the student will work toward remaining in her seat or other designated spot during silent reading time—which is the twenty minutes following lunch recess (short period of time following a physical-release outlet offers greatest chance of success). Success will earn her a token toward computer time, a movie pass or some other end result that is attractive to her.

For most children, experiencing success results in positive momentum. As her successes build, her frustration will ebb, and so will the upsetting outbursts.

• Disappointment

Disappointment comes when someone he counted upon didn't come through; an event anticipated didn't happen. While a typically-developing child may be able to roll with the punches when schedules or events change, the child with autism depends mightily upon routine and familiarity. Accommodating abrupt changes of direction in his day requires skills he may not yet have and can cause disruption from which it can take hours to recover. Disappointment is a matter of degree for every individual, and it may be a very tough sled to arrive at the point where you understand and empathize with your child's perspective. To you, it's a blip in the routine; to him, a malevolent threat to emotional equilibrium. Some disappointments will be utterly unpredictable: the store is out of his favorite ice cream, the usual route to school is detoured because of road repair, his TV show is preempted for a breaking news report, a playdate is cancelled because Sarah is sick. Others can be circumvented with careful forethought and planning: tell him the pool at this year's vacation hotel will not have a diving board and show him a picture from the hotel brochure or website, have Grandma tell him she will be serving apple pie instead of pumpkin at Thanksgiving this year, explain that Calvin the beloved Camp Counselor won't be back this year but go to meet Nathan the New Guy before the session starts.

- Maltreatment

She is being attacked, provoked or teased by peers, siblings or other adults. Whether in your home, your school or any other setting, there is only one acceptable position: no tolerance. How user-friendly is your child's environment in this regard? If the attitude is, "Well, kids can be cruel, that's just the way it is," know with certainty that your child with autism has neither the verbal sophistication nor the social acuity to adequately defend herself. Angry meltdowns are only the beginning. Close on their heels may be anxiety, depression and chronic fatigue. Taking action to protect your child or student in such situations is mandatory.

Our elementary school's administration and teaching staff ferociously enforced a policy declaring the school a No Put-Down Zone. Incidences of unkindness in any shade were dealt with promptly and decisively. We never took our school's policy for granted, not for a minute. At another school, a mother told me a different story:

He started first-grade with positive, consistent feedback from us, but quickly deteriorated under physical abuse from his peers on an almost daily basis. Both the teacher's and the principal's reactions to my repeated concerns were that I just needed to stop being so overprotective. My son needed to learn how to take care of himself; these things just happen between kids and you can't always be there to save them! He needed to learn to stand up for himself, stop being such a baby, focus more, work harder, listen better, do as told, try harder, be more responsive, and on, and on, and on.

I crumble inside every time I hear a shameful account such as this one. "These things just happen between kids"? Of course they do—if the adults in charge continue to allow it! Whether the perpetrators are classmates, siblings or other adults, our choosing to take no action is in fact a choice: to allow harassment to flourish. And if the victim's response is anger or aggression— duh!!!

So here's the chant again: just because he can't tell you it's happening doesn't mean that it isn't. Be aware that most harassment happens out of the hearing range of parents, teachers and other adults: on the bus, in the bathroom, in the halls, on the playground. Teach your child or student, as soon as he is able, to 1) protest appropriately, "Stop! I don't like that!" and 2) tell a trusted adult.

- Sense of unfairness

"Fair" is one of those hazy, imprecise terms that is very perplexing to our kids with autism. He doesn't think in terms of fair or unfair, but does know he's having trouble balancing his needs with the rules. As parents, teachers or coaches, we generally think of "fair" as meaning impartial, even-handed, equitable, unbiased. Family rules, school rules and team rules apply to each sibling, student or teammate equally. But autism "un-levels" the playing field. It potholes the field. All things are not being equal. So our thinking on the subject of "fair" must change. Here it is:

"Fair" does not mean everything is absolutely equal.

"Fair" is when everyone gets what they need.

4. Poor examples from adults

I once worked for a general manager who would occasionally invoke a patently indelicate metaphor when he wanted to place responsibility in someone else's lap. He didn't care for the usual sports idioms like, "The ball is in their court." Rather, he liked to "put the turd back in their pocket." It always turned a few ears pink and set off a gag reflex or two. Vivid, unpleasant imagery, but sometimes that's what it takes to focus attention on something from which we'd rather turn away.

The mirror can be unforgiving, but any examination of our child's undesirable behavior has to start with a look at our own. "Speak when you are angry and you will make the best speech you'll ever regret," said Laurence J. Peter, author of *The Peter Principle: Why Things Always Go Wrong.* If you are reacting with anger and frustration to your child or student's meltdowns, you are modeling the very behavior you want him or her to change. It is incumbent upon you as an adult, at all times and in every situation, to absolutely refrain from responding in kind. Try to figure out what triggers your own boiling point—be your own behavior detective—and interrupt the episode before you reach that point. When your thermostat zooms skyward, better to temporarily remove yourself from the situation. Tell your child: "You are angry [frustrated, upset] and I am, too. I need to be away from you [or, by myself] for a few minutes so that I can calm down. I am going to my room [or outside or upstairs] for now, but I will come back to you and we can talk about it."

There are lots of ways in which we unwittingly make a bad situation worse. Derision is laughing at someone's pain or misfortune, projecting a "that serves you right!" attitude. Sometimes we make unfair, irrelevant comparisons—"Your sister never did this." Then there are so-called kitchen-sink arguments, bringing up bygone incidents: "This is just like the time you ____." We may make unproven accusations: "You must have done this. Nobody else would have." As with any difficult situation, good planning helps immeasurably. At a time when you are calm, think through how you can better handle the next incident. Then write down your plan, keep it in an accessible place, and refer to it periodically to keep it fresh in your mind.

And finally, we cannot end a discussion about anger without raising the most difficult issue.

There are very few black-and-whites in raising children, and even fewer in raising a child with ASD. But here is one: never, ever is there an instance when it is acceptable to hit a child. My guess is that most readers who have come this far into this book are not so inclined anyway. I've got your back here; consider what follows to be your ammo against that vocal family member, neighbor or bystander who feels the pressing need to let you know that all your kid needs is a good smack.

You can put lipstick on this pig by calling it "spanking," "swatting," "paddling," or "corporal punishment," but the bottom line is, it is an aggressive act perpetrated almost invariably in anger. Sometimes it happens in a momentary loss of self-control, sometimes with the mistaken conviction that it will somehow, without the actual effort of instruction, teach better behavior. Consider:

- Do we spank after careful weighing of alternative responses and calmly deciding that, yes, striking someone one-quarter our size is logical, provides a good example for them to follow and will produce the desired long-term result? Can we be sure that it actually teaches the child what she did wrong and how to correct the behavior? Or do we spank out of aggravation, wrath and desperation? Does it foster respect and understanding—or humiliation and bewilderment? Is it a behavior you want the child to emulate?

- The same behavior perpetrated toward a coworker or neighbor would be called "assault and battery," possibly earning you a free ride in the squad car. Under the Geneva conventions, we are not even allowed to do it to prisoners of war. Why should it be okay to do it to a child?

Our pediatrician told us: Spanking is like smoking. If you never start, you won't have to worry about quitting. Because if you do start, when and where do you stop? If you spank for this, what about that? The headstrong child may develop a tolerance to it—do you escalate the penalty? If you do, where does it end?

Anger is contagious, and in the end, it costs you—in time lost, energy expended, trust violated, self-worth stunted, feelings wounded and long term results unattained. Yet, anger is also inevitable in the human experience. Learning to handle anger with proactive self-control and dignity ultimately empowers both you and, through your example, your child.

Ferreting out the causes and consequences of troubling behaviors has a formal name. A *Functional Behavior Analysis* (FBA) begins by assessing specific behaviors based on their "ABCs": the *antecedent* or cause/trigger, the *behavior* itself and the *consequence* or what happens to the child as a result of the behavior. An FBA can be a formal process (i.e., carried out in the school setting by trained personnel) or informal one (i.e., parental home observation). There are many good books and websites that can guide you through the process. The idea behind an FBA is that, once identified, the antecedents and consequences of a behavior can be altered or modified in a manner that redirects the child to more appropriate behavior. That's such an important piece of the equation that I am going to repeat it: behavior modification doesn't stop at interrupting or extinguishing an undesirable behavior. *Redirecting the child to appropriate replacement behavior* is name of the endgame. However baffling or distasteful to you, his behavior is happening for a reason and is filling a need; vanquishing a behavior without filling the underlying need yields net zero.

I would never suggest that learning to deal with your child's meltdowns is easy. But it is most definitely one piece of the autism puzzle where there are answers to be had for those who are up for the search. I myself found the process a bit wondrous. The better I got at identifying *and respecting* Bryce's triggers, the more peaceful life became. The frightening several-times-a-day meltdowns diminished to several times a week, morphed briefly into occasional passive-aggressive responses, then vanished completely. Completely. It's been many years since I've thought about it in any manner other than being grateful for how we were able to confront and face down something so ugly. My recall of those bad old days is fading. It's one of the most impressive special effects I've ever seen.

Chapter Ten

Love me unconditionally.

"The difference between heaven and earth is not so much *altitude* but *attitude*."

These words come from the book *The Power of Unconditional Love* by Ken Keys, Jr. They are the strong overarching sentiment for everything I believe about raising a child with autism, and they come from a man who lived it every day. Keys used a wheelchair the last fifty years of his life, owing to polio, so he knew a little about living with a so-called disability. It sure didn't stop him from writing prolifically—fifteen books—about loving life, finding happiness in what you already have and keeping your focus forward. He makes the very thought-provoking observation that unconditional love is based on dualities, the most encompassing of which is that to truly love someone else, we have to love ourselves. What that ultimately means is "accepting all parts of ourselves." What better example to set for your child?

I do believe unconditional love is both magical and attainable. I wrote about it in my Mother's and Father's Day column in 2005:

> There is no question whatever that the challenges of raising atypical children can seem staggering. Face in the dirt, knife in the heart, down for the count. But it's always been my privilege to claim our two boys as mine and to love them unconditionally. It's taught me profound lessons about how excruciating it can be to keep

that kind of love in the crosshairs at all times. You, too? Rising above and firmly pushing aside our own fears, disappointments, expectations and lost dreams can seem like a mission of overwhelming enormity. Your child's limitations become your limitations—the places you can't take him, the social settings he can't handle, the people he can't relate to, the food he won't eat. Yeah, it can be a long list.

It takes great courage to admit that you are scared, feel cheated, heartsick, depleted. Wanting out of that matrix and not knowing how to start. Here's how you start: by knowing you can do this. It's already in you.

In the beginning, as I contemplated what Bryce's life and my family's would be like with autism in our midst, I could not deny the fact that it could be so much worse. All around me were people who had confronted just that. Close friends had lost their precious two-year-old daughter to a heart defect. It was a life-shattering event and it was much, much worse than anything autism ever threw at me and my family.

Bryce taught me that happiness does not come from getting what you want, but from wanting what you already have. It is the greatest gift I have ever been given. A friend once asked me: But how do you get there? What do you think is the secret of your success?

It's no secret. It is just this: As much as possible, accept your situation without bitterness. Play the cards you drew with grace and optimism. Bitterness can be a formidable foe; overcoming it can be a daily exercise. Some of us make it, some of us don't.

Back in chapter three, I spoke of a parent who claimed that because of autism, he could not have a relationship with his son. He "knew" his son was going to end up in prison. I talked and reasoned and pleaded away the afternoon with this man, begging him to see that he was setting up a self-fulfilling prophecy:

> *Couldn't he take one baby step out, imagining a different outcome for his belligerent but very bright child – ten minutes of floor time, coming to school once a month, finding a restaurant only the two of them liked? I think he loved his son but to the child it no doubt felt conditional, dependent upon a certain kind of behavior, even if there were organic reasons why he could not comply. In the end, they both lost out. This dad could not move beyond his bitterness and grief.*

> *Grief is real. But getting stuck in that grief—that is the true tragedy, not the fact that your child has autism.*

> *Unconditional love means removing the qualifiers, directing the focus of autism's difficulties away from yourself. Neither you nor he chose that he should have autism. But remember: it is happening to him, not you. I can testify that walking with your child in his shoes will liberate both of you. For me, understanding sensory integration propelled me out of my own fears. I was horrified by the knowledge of what Bryce was living with: his prison of environmental hostility, having no "normal" basis of comparison, never knowing that life can be something other than a bombardment of unpleasant sensations. He was very young, without life experience and without means of communicating his misery. I could not turn away from the raw truth, which was this:*

If I do not swallow my own anguish and be the one to step up for him, who will?

Think of your own child or student and try to imagine his world: the incessant sensory invasion, the eddies of incomprehensible language swirling around him, the impatience and disregard of "normal" people. You face the same question I did: if not you—who?

Do you even dare imagine his life as an adult after you are gone? That's a harsh question, and it's the one that keeps me on track every day of my life. What kind of life awaits an adult who has limited language ability, doesn't comprehend the law and law enforcement, the banking system, public transportation, workplace issues such as punctuality, basic etiquette? To what level of quality can life rise without a meaningful interpersonal relationship or two, meaningful work and the ability to enjoy meaningful pastimes or hobbies? Neuro-typicals assume that these things will be the components of their adult lives. For the child with autism, such a future can exist, but not without the deliberate intervention of adults committed 100% to the idea that being all and everything we can be is the birthright of every child. My column continued:

For some cosmic, not-to-be-understood reason, I was blessed with the serenity to bypass the denial and the anger and the self-pity that frequently come unbidden and unwelcome when we learn our child has a disability. But that is not to say that I don't endure my own bouts with melancholy. I never, ever fail to be deeply hurt by what I call the Knife to the Heart moments. These are the times when the rest of the world seems intent on letting you know that your child is different and apart. Usually there's no conscious malice; it just happens because the "typical" population is steaming about their business in "typical" fashion that doesn't or can't include your child. The offhand child-cruel remark, the birthday party that everyone else is invited to, the snubs on the bus, the questions he asks you as he begins to figure out that he is different. I always thought that if I endured enough Knife to the Heart moments, I would develop scar tissue or the ability to laugh them off. I haven't. But as both my boys move with increasing grace toward maturity and independence, the Knife to the Heart moments become fewer, farther between and more fleeting. The power I allowed them to have over me has weakened over time.

Loving Bryce unconditionally required, at different times, making peace with what seemed like reduced opportunities. He didn't seem to want conventional friendships, play dates and sleepovers, wasn't interested in the usual after-school activities like soccer or choir. He couldn't tolerate large-scale shows like Sesame Street Live, Ice Capades or the circus. Travel had to be carefully orchestrated. Curiously, I can't say I missed these things because he plainly was a happy child who felt good about himself. Still I pondered. And still I asked a lot of questions:

There I sat one morning in our psychologist's office, bewildered yet again at my son's social development, which seemed to meander all over the landscape without ever really treading the "path." During this memorable meeting, I received the greatest advice he ever gave me. After the practical and the actionable suggestions, he added, "And remember: all children, all people, unfold in their own time. This may just not be his time. His time will come."

And I was determined to give him the time and space to do just that. Those times did come. As he grew older, he swam on a swim team and ran on the track team, became a rather accomplished actor in community theater, surfed and backpacked, zoomed around on his bike, enjoyed Cub Scout activities, read Harry Potter. And he did it right on time—his time. It may have been a couple of years behind the "typical" timeline, but he did it just as successfully as any kid, and what's more, the minute he did—we magically forgot that he ever hadn't.

Every day of Bryce's life I have told him that he is the best kid who ever lived, that I am the luckiest mommy who ever lived, that he is great just the way he is. In the beginning, I believed it just enough to start saying it, but as time went on a wonderful thing happened. It became fact to me. More importantly, it became fact to him. And because he believes it, he has grown into a young man with remarkable aplomb, self-confidence, empathy and work ethic—not necessarily the typical hallmarks of autism. He has built marvelous self-esteem; he likes himself and is comfortable with who he is. It was contagious; I began to actively look for things about him to articulate: I told him I was proud of how readily he shared treats and privileges with others, how I admired his devotion to his school work, how much I enjoyed the clever associations he made as he pulled minute details out of movies and related them to his real life. How much I could trust him because he never lied, how nicely he took care of himself with healthy food choices and good hygiene.

Think of it as affirmative brainwashing—the more you tell your child he's the greatest, the more both of you are going to believe it.

If you can get to a place where you believe, accept and put true unconditional love into practice, you will find yourself infused with an incredible energy on behalf of your child. It's that powerful. Without it, you are going to be running this race with a fairly nasty pebble in your shoe. It may be a $100 shoe, but that pebble will ensure that your focus dwells on the ever more painful wound to your extremity, rather than on the span of the road ahead or the beauty of your surroundings. It's a pretty simple choice: let the irritant remain until it cripples you, or remove it and head for the horizon.

With the full force of your commitment behind the rudder, your child's time will come.

The fast track, high speed, express lane, maximum velocity, instant results, record pace, immediate gratification culture of the 21st century is not the hand your child drew. He or she is leading you down that road less traveled, the road the poet Frost himself tells us is "just as fair, and having perhaps the better claim." It is perhaps the better claim because, at the end of this book, we have come full circle, back to where we started: neither you nor he yet know what the scope of his achievement can be, river deep, mountain high. We can't see the end of the road, not only because it is full of dips and slopes and tricky curves, but because there is no end. An energizing, uplifting thought, or a draining, wearying one—your choice. Henry Ford, that icon of American industrialism, succeeded in spectacular fashion largely because he sought out people "who have an infinite capacity to not know what can't be done."

I want to leave you with the deeply wise words of Joshua Liebman's *A Parent's Commandments.* Our family committed to these directives at the naming ceremonies we held for both of our sons shortly after their births. They were happy occasions during which everything seemed possible for our child(ren), and we could never have imagined how prescient these words would be:

"Give your child unconditional love,
a love that is not dependent on report cards,
clean hands or popularity.

Give your child a sense of your whole-hearted acceptance,
acceptance of his human frailties as well as his
abilities and virtues.

Give him a sense of truth; make him aware of himself as a
citizen of the universe in which there are many obstacles
as well as fulfillments.

Give your child permission to grow up and make
their own life independent of you.
These are the laws of honoring your child."

Please join me in doing this for your child. Along your road less traveled, it will make all the difference.

Forward . . .

The "forward" typically comes at the beginning of a book, and this is the part that's supposed to be called the "conclusion." But our trek is not typical. And we are really closer to the beginning than the end of the adventure, so it seems more appropriate to continue to look *forward* and ahead, past the last page. The journey is circular anyway. One of Bryce's paraeducators, a professional of many years' experience, looked back on her years with Bryce and told me, "All that time I thought I was teaching him but now I see it was really he who was teaching me." I feel the same way. *Ten Things* only scratches the surface of what I have learned from Bryce. But there is a certain core of thought to which I always seem to return like a boomerang.

"Whether you think you can or whether you think you can't, you are probably right." That's Henry Ford again, a person who arguably occupied a spot somewhere on the autism/Asperger's/ADHD spectrum. An authentic diagnosis is lost to history, but the diagnosis is so much less important than the message: what you choose to believe about your child's autism is possibly the single biggest factor in the outcome.

If that sounds like a challenge—it is. Run with it; the wind is definitely at your back. It will keep you moving forward; that's where the action is and where the answers are. *Why* your child has autism may be a question without an answer, but *what* you can do about it, *how* you can make a difference and *where* to seek the resources to guide you are questions with concrete answers that will keep you going for the rest of your life.

It doesn't matter a bit how you get to the point of being a Believer. I myself sometimes can't *believe* how I got there. But it's a great story, my own personal parable, so I am going to share:

Even though I am well past forty, I am going back to school. I'll be studying at my beloved old alma mater and it's wonderful to be back. In over twenty years, very little that I originally loved about it has changed. It's still a little strip of a town. It still has its quaint square for a downtown.

But there's a kink in my homecoming. And it's literally about home. Even though I started looking months in advance, I can't nail down an apartment. One is supposed to be available but when I come with my stuff, someone is already living there. Another turns out to be on the far side of nowhere and it's cramped, dilapidated and stinky. One landlord wants me to wait two weeks; there might be an availability. Finally, the term is starting and there is nothing, just me and my car. I'm too old for dormitory life but I've run out of options. The dorms are fully booked, I'm told, but I can stay in this one room until the student with the reservation shows up.

Thus begins a harrowing game of human checkers as I am moved from room to room every few days, clearing out for the next legitimate name on the waiting list, moving to a space temporarily vacated by the latest dropout. When I get shoved one last time to the end unit of this tenuous tenement, will I simply fall out the hall window and vanish into the Vinca major?

But I have another problem, just as bad. With all the constant distraction of my homelessness, the term is suddenly half over. I've skipped some classes—well, actually, a lot of classes. In shock, I realize that it is too late to recover by the end of the term. By missing so much class, I don't have the background to complete the coursework and I have no relationships with the professors upon which to fall back and possibly create alternative solutions. I am going to fail—resoundingly—for the first time in my academic career. It is humiliation on a level I could never have imagined.

And then I wake up.

The dream is more curious than disturbing, because it keeps popping up every few months. Its message seems so consistent. I check out some books on dream interpretation from the library, but I find nothing to explain the lack-of-housing component.

An easy-going acquaintance of mine, who seems so down-to-earth in every other way, urges me to go see a professional psychic she knows. Laurie could figure it out in a snap, she says, and wouldn't it be nice to know? What if it is something important?

Laurie, it turned out, was a former critical care nurse who now ran a thriving psychic consultancy. She had a large number of business clients on retainers and she conducted extensive workshops on topics such as hypnotherapy and past life regression. Her office was in an upscale suburb. My curiosity finally won out and I made an appointment for a reading.

She begins the session by telling me, "Don't say anything yet. I will tell you what I'm getting from you, and then there will be plenty of time to ask questions." For the first five minutes, she tells me things she couldn't possibly know. Okay, she's authentic and I am mighty impressed. Now we can get to the question about my dream. She brushes it off in a matter of seconds. "That one's easy," she said. "You are looking for greater intellectual stimulation but can't figure out how to fit it into your life—

I see a book published within the next five years."

Yes, and I'll become an Olympic decathlete, too, I think. It's not what I was expecting, but it's interesting and I press on. I want to ask you about my child, I start hesitantly. There seems to be something—extra—about him. She looks at his photo and asks for his birth date.

It's kind of scary, I manage to get out. Is he an angel or a fairy or something?

Oh no, she says. Not an angel. An angel is a new soul. He is a very old soul.

She starts to talk about past life regression, and I listen impassively. Do I believe this stuff? No, I can't say that I do. But then, neither do I *not* believe it. Nobody has ever proven anything to me one way or the other. I've paid my money and I'm here looking for answers so I might as well listen with an open mind.

Bryce is a great spiritual leader, she says. You and he have been together many times in many lifetimes, in different roles: teacher and student, husband and wife, leader and confidante. He trusts you. This time, you are here together as mother and son. This is the role he chose for you. This time.

"He chose me?"

"Yes."

Laurie gives me a tape of our session. Go home and let everything percolate and sift and settle for a few weeks, she says. Then listen to this again.

So that's what I do. It's hard not be mesmerized by the idea—which, remember, I don't quite believe—that he chose me. One night, an entirely ordinary bedtime, we are ending the day in the usual way, on his bed with a book. It's been a busy summer day filled with camp and popsicles and grass stains. He's a clear and pleasant tired; it's not going to be an hour of long goodnights. Heavy eyelids are descending over his famous blue eyes. In the purplish-gray light, the curve of his cheek and nose and the plane of his skin seem beyond real. I know it's unfair and unfitting, but I can't resist, can't fight it. I have to ask him.

"Bryce?"

"Yes?" It's an all-but-asleep whisper.

"Did you choose me?"

By his silence, I think he has drifted off. Then, though his eyes do not open, I hear quite clearly:

"Yes, Mom."

Have you ever in your life been confronted with something that caused you to simply evacuate your senses? It was certainly a moment forever apart for me because *I did not know what to think.*

Of course he could have just been tired and wanting me to leave. But I heard something else. I heard it through the haze of my own long-standing skepticism.

What I heard was that there was a lot more "choice" at stake than whether or not there was any verifiable truth in the scenario of him choosing me as a mother. The larger significance lies in what we choose to believe even where no tangible evidence exists, and how we will allow that choosing to direct our actions.

When beloved American composer George Gershwin passed away, the novelist John O'Hara said, "George died on July 11, 1937, but I don't have to believe that if I don't want to."

We choose to believe that which provides us with what we need to make it through the tough situations. Allowing myself to believe that Bryce had in fact chosen me as his mother renewed my determination to do right by him. It was such an enormous thought, that somehow across time, he believed that I was the one for the job. If this was true, our belief in each other was eternally circular.

"Whether you think you can or whether you think you can't, you are probably right."

A spectrum's worth of personal difference and 100 years' time separate Laurie's remarks from Henry Ford's. So disparate are they that the only way they could both have ended up in my lap together is that they are bound by a common truth: that it is choice, not chance, that guides our hand on the helm.

I believe that.

Note to non-believers: Laurie's remark, "I see a book published in the next five years," was pretty startling. Such a thought had never crossed my mind. Almost two years to the day after that conversation, I began writing about my experiences with Bryce. Three-and-a-half years after that conversation, my first book, 1001 Great Ideas for Teaching and Raising Children with Autism Spectrum Disorders, *was published.*

Acknowledgements

My thanks go first to Steve Boehm, editor-in-chief of *Children's Voice* and Vicki McCash Brennan, managing editor of *South Florida Parenting*, publishers of the original "Ten Things" article, and to their thousands of readers, so many of whom wrote and still write to share their thoughts. Their stories are heartbreaking, inspiring, frustrating, uplifting and motivating, and every one of them touches me.

Special thanks to my publisher Wayne Gilpin, for giving me another opportunity to be part of the tremendous ripple effect Future Horizons creates, spreading know-how and can-do across the autism community.

Every writer deserves a real live muse, but not every writer is lucky enough to have one. This book would be a far paler shade of itself without the talent, guidance and sisterhood of Veronica Zysk. I am beyond grateful.

My mother Henny and my husband Mark, with their two-word vocabularies ("Terrific! Wonderful!") are hopeless as editors, but as a rally squad they are formidable. Could I have written this book without their fail-safe support? Maybe, but I'm so glad I'll never have to find out.

Without my boys, my own personal superheroes, there is, of course, no book. Connor and Bryce: against all statistical odds I got you, the two greatest humans on the planet. You are the delightful, consummate embodiment of the words of one of my own favorite authors, Mark Twain: "My mother had a lot of trouble with me, but I think she rather enjoyed it!"

About the author

Book author, columnist and mother of sons with autism and AD/HD, Ellen Notbohm writes extensively on autism, baseball and genealogy. A columnist for *Autism Asperger's Digest*, she co-authored the award-winning *1001 Great Ideas for Teaching and Raising Children with Autism Spectrum Disorders.*

A note from Ellen:

Your feedback as a reader is of great importance to me. The thoughts and theories, the feelings and philosophies of my readers all around the world are the current that carried Ten Things *along from a humble magazine article to the book it has now become. Your comments are welcome at:*

ellen_notbohm@comcast.net.

More award-winning titles by Ellen Notbohm!

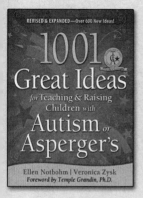

Winner of Learning Magazine's Teachers Choice Award, the first edition of 1001 Great Ideas has been a treasured resource in the autism community since 2004. Now, in this expanded edition, Ellen Notbohm and Veronica Zysk present parents and educators with over 1800 ideas try-it-now tips, eye-opening advice, and grassroots strategies. More than 600 fresh ideas join tried and true tactics from the original edition, while many ideas pick up where the first edition left off, offering modifications for older kids, honing in on Asperger's challenges, and enhancing already-effective ways to help your child or student achieve success at home, in school, and in the community. Don't let tradition and habit stand in the way of what your child or student can do!

ISBN 9781935274063 $24.95

The unique perspective of a child's voice returns to help us understand the thinking patterns that guide their actions, shape an environment conducive to their learning style, and communicate with them in meaningful ways. It's the game plan every educator, parent, or family member needs to make the most of every "teaching moment" in the life of these children we love. Winner of an iParenting Media Award and Finalist in the 2006 ForeWord Book of the Year Awards!

ISBN 9781932565362 $14.95

"Do not go where the path may lead, go instead where there is no path and leave a trail." —Ralph Waldo Emerson.

In a cohesive compilation of her best articles, Ellen offers advice on concrete issues such as math homework, video games, and tricky behavior, and also tackles the more abstract concepts of parenting: trusting parental instincts, when to take risks, how to hang on, and when to let go. Finalist in the 2007 ForeWord Book of the Year Awards and finalist in the 2008 Eric Hoffer Awards, this book is absolutely invaluable to all who are "on the autism trail."

ISBN 9781932565508 $19.95

"" Ellen captures the major issues of autism and makes them understandable and usable, even to those new to spectrum disorders .... ""

Nancy Cale, Vice President of Unlocking Autism

Available in bookstores everywhere!

Madelyne
Diaz
Madelyne Diaz

Madelyne
Diaz